T0036629

HABITS
FOR A
SACRED
HOME

BOOKS BY JENNIFER PEPITO

Mothering by the Book
Habits for a Sacred Home

"*Habits for a Sacred Home* is destined to become a classic. Deep, insightful thoughts that give clarity to a biblical vision for home, children, family, and mission are clearly defined in the pages of this perceptive book. Jennifer is a seasoned woman and has gleaned wisdom through many aspects of life. She writes with authority. All women who long to follow God, and to be filled with courage, should read this book. I was inspired and motivated to keep following hard after God in His calling on my own life. Excellent in every way."

—Sally Clarkson, author of many books, podcast host (*At Home with Sally*), mother of four adult children, and one who has sought to build a sacred home

"Jennifer Pepito combines her love of learning with her passion for motherhood in this inspiring collection of anecdotes and insightful practices. A time-traveler's guide to the saints and heroes of the faith, this book shows us practical ways to experience the sacred in the simple, everyday moments of life."

—Ainsley Arment, founder of Wild + Free

"*Habits for a Sacred Home* offers the hard-earned, compassionate wisdom our homes need right now. Drawing upon the rich, diverse histories of the Benedictines and other pillars of our faith, Jennifer Pepito challenges women to push back on the darkness and decay of this world by employing a few simple practices in our days."

—Jamie Erickson, author of *Holy Hygge*, co-host of the *Mom to Mom Podcast*

"In *Habits for a Sacred Home*, Jennifer Pepito invites us to explore the profound difference that life-giving rhythms can make in our homes and families. With powerful stories of inspiring women of faith and practical steps to determine your family values, this book will serve as a trusted guide to help you create and cultivate better habits that ultimately lead to a more peace-filled, purposeful home and life."

—Crystal Paine, *New York Times* bestselling author, mom of six, podcast host, and founder of MoneySavingMom.com

"In a world that often feels chaotic and demanding, *Habits for a Sacred Home* serves as a beacon of wisdom and solace. Jennifer Pepito's words emphasize the importance of recognizing our limitations and surrendering to the love and goodness of God. This book is not just a read; it's an invitation to create a space that nourishes our souls."

—Ginny Yurich, bestselling author, podcast host, and founder of 1000 Hours Outside

"For every parent seeking a return to the basics, here's your compass. By shedding light on nine tried-and-true habits formed in the homes of history's most trailblazing women, Jennifer Pepito illuminates the way toward a simpler, truer life for us all—one that is void of current controversies and trend-driven assumptions, but instead unveils the rich and foundational depth that comes from prioritizing what matters most."

—Erin Loechner, bestselling author of *The Opt-Out Family*
and founder of Other Goose

"Jennifer Pepito's voice is so needed in this generation—the voice of a seasoned mother who both admits her struggles and points us toward the source of hope and truth: Jesus. In *Habits for a Sacred Home*, Jennifer lays out helpful, practical, biblical principles, interwoven with her own stories of God's grace, for recentering our homes around truth, beauty, and peace when the clamor of our culture threatens to overwhelm us."

—Abbie Halberstadt, mother, influencer, and author of *M Is for Mama* and *Hard Is Not the Same Thing as Bad*

"*Habits for a Sacred Home* intricately intertwines faith and family, tracing a journey from Benedict to Bethune. Through shared meals and ancient prayers, Jennifer Pepito creates a tapestry of joy, intentional living, and practical wisdom. Beyond being a compelling read, it serves as a guiding companion, enriching the sacred fabric of family life with transformative habits."

—Leah Boden, author of *Modern Miss Mason*

"Jennifer has such a gift for knowing what her readers need next. After sharing in her first book how she overcame many of the lies she was taught, the groundwork was set to begin cultivating the habits of restoration found in her newest book, *Habits for a Sacred Home*. Jennifer's truth telling is loving, and her teaching style is hands-on, yet approachable for all to achieve."

—Kate Crocco, LCSW, author of *Thinking Like a Boss* and
Drawing the Line and host of the *Thinking Like a Boss Podcast*

"Jennifer Pepito's elegant invitation to live well offers renewed hope for mothers. She captures long-held fears for our families and our world and covers them with truth. I'm more inspired than ever to follow the path of everyday women who have gone before me as hardworking, benevolent stewards and waymakers."

—Amber O'Neal Johnston, author of *A Place to Belong*
and curator of HeritageMom.com

HABITS
FOR A
SACRED
HOME

9 PRACTICES FROM HISTORY TO ANCHOR AND RESTORE MODERN FAMILIES

JENNIFER PEPITO

BETHANYHOUSE

a division of Baker Publishing Group
Minneapolis, Minnesota

© 2024 by Jennifer Pepito

Published by Bethany House Publishers
Minneapolis, Minnesota
BethanyHouse.com

Bethany House Publishers is a division of
Baker Publishing Group, Grand Rapids, Michigan

Printed in the United States of America

All rights reserved. No part of this publication may be reproduced, stored in a retrieval system, or transmitted in any form or by any means—for example, electronic, photocopy, recording—without the prior written permission of the publisher. The only exception is brief quotations in printed reviews.

Library of Congress Cataloging-in-Publication Data
Names: Pepito, Jennifer, author.
Title: Habits for a sacred home : 9 practices from history to anchor and restore modern families / Jennifer Pepito.
Description: Minneapolis, Minnesota : Bethany House, a division of Baker Publishing Group, [2024] | Includes bibliographical references.
Identifiers: LCCN 2023049991 | ISBN 9780764239540 (paperback) | ISBN 9780764243318 (casebound) | ISBN 9781493446728 (ebook)
Subjects: LCSH: Families—Religious aspects—Christianity.
Classification: LCC BV4526.3 .P47 2024 | DDC 248.4—dc23/eng/20231221
LC record available at https://lccn.loc.gov/2023049991

Unless otherwise indicated, Scripture quotations are from The Holy Bible, English Standard Version® (ESV®), copyright © 2001 by Crossway, a publishing ministry of Good News Publishers. Used by permission. All rights reserved. ESV Text Edition: 2016

Scripture quotations labeled ASV are from the American Standard Version of the Bible

Scripture quotations labeled KJV are from the King James Version of the Bible.

Scripture quotations labeled NIV are from THE HOLY BIBLE, NEW INTERNATIONAL VERSION®, NIV® Copyright © 1973, 1978, 1984, 2011 by Biblica, Inc.® Used by permission. All rights reserved worldwide.

Scripture quotations labeled NKJV are from the New King James Version®. Copyright © 1982 by Thomas Nelson. Used by permission. All rights reserved.

The recipes included in each chapter are from The Peaceful Press Cookbook: Recipes for a Living Education by Jennifer Pepito, © 2023 by The Peaceful Press. Used by permission.

Cover design by Micah Kandros Design
Cover Image: Creative Market, Rachel Kick
Author photo © Brooke Battle

Published in association with The Bindery Agency, www.TheBinderyAgency.com.

Baker Publishing Group publications use paper produced from sustainable forestry practices and postconsumer waste whenever possible.

24 25 26 27 28 29 30   7 6 5 4 3 2 1

To my mother, Rosalind, and my sisters
Jacqueline, Jody, Tammi, and LeeAnn
Your faithfulness to your families is an inspiration to the world.
You are creating restoration homes.

CONTENTS

1

THE NEED FOR
SACRED HOMES

Stand in the ways and see,
And ask for the old paths, where the good way is,
And walk in it;
Then you will find rest for your souls.

Jeremiah 6:16 NKJV

I finished cleaning the kitchen after our family dinner and devotions and took a quick scroll through my phone while I got ready for bed. It had become a little routine to pick up my phone for a few minutes each evening before settling in with a book. Some of my end-of-the-day phone time was legitimate; a quick check-in with my community on Instagram and a text to my out-of-town son were essential communications for me. But this time I also snuck in a few minutes on Twitter, with a twinge of guilt as I entered the URL. I'd worked so hard to overcome fear, and I knew that looking at the bad news on Twitter was not going to help me stay fearless. The provocative posts could never kindle the hope that I needed to mother well.

I scanned the headlines with growing horror: a tech executive stabbed to death while walking home in San Francisco, vicious terror attacks in the Middle East, war in Europe, and toxic levels of aluminum in local rainwater. Although I had worked hard to overcome fear and wrote about that process in *Mothering by the Book*, the world felt frightening, and I was searching for wisdom to guide my family through rapidly changing times.

The state of the world was a frequent conversation with friends as well. Some, who believed the Lord was coming back any day, kept their normal routines in hopes of being raptured out. Other friends believed we were on the verge of the Great Tribulation, and moved their families closer to like-minded communities to strategize how they could grow enough food to supply themselves when everything fell apart. I also have friends whose eschatology points to the world getting better before the return of Christ, so they are going about their business, joining committees, leading mission trips, and not paying too much attention to the headlines.

I wasn't holding my breath to be raptured out anytime soon, but I didn't know what to believe. I'm a panmillennialist; I believe in the personal and physical return of Jesus Christ, but I don't really know how it will all "pan" out. I don't know if his return will be pre-tribulation or post-tribulation, or if we are in the millennium now. This lack of certainty about what is going on in the world was unsettling. When a string of fires destroyed food packing plants, I wondered if we should buy emergency food supplies. When prominent European banks collapsed, I wondered if we would lose our savings. I was on high alert trying to navigate a rapidly changing world and keep my children safe, and the more I consumed frightening news, the more uncomfortable I felt in my own skin. My fears weren't baseless, but there had to be a better way to live.

A Better Way

In the midst of navigating my response to the news, I read a book called *The Benedict Option* by Rod Dreher. In it, Dreher highlights the life of Saint Benedict (AD 480–547) and the path he took when Roman civilization was falling around him. Instead of merely adapting to the culture and reshaping his beliefs to conform to new moral dilemmas, he separated himself from the culture to be with God. For three years he lived alone in a cave, nurturing his devotion to Jesus. He counted being in the presence of the Lord of greater worth than the pleasures of Rome. Reflecting on the saint's life, Pope Gregory wrote that Benedict, "desiring rather the miseries of the world than the praises of men, rather to be wearied with labour for God's sake than to be exalted with transitory commendation, fled privily from his nurse, and went into a desert place called Subiaco."[1]

Because of his devotion, Benedict's fame grew, and soon he had gathered a number of people around him who dwelled in similar dedication to God. They lived an orderly, balanced life of work and prayer, and when Roman civilization descended into chaos, they built a new community based on a biblical rule of life. Dreher points to a similar prescription for us today. Instead of continuing to fight against the culture or trying to "save America," perhaps it is time to simply pursue a godly life and practice benevolent detachment, releasing the state of the world to God and living according to his Word despite what is happening around us. Dreher writes,

> Today we can see that we've lost on every front and that the swift and relentless currents of secularism have overwhelmed our flimsy barriers. . . .
>
> Could it be that the best way to fight the flood is to . . . stop fighting the flood? That is, to quit piling up sandbags and to build an ark in which to shelter until the water recedes and we can put our feet on dry land again? Rather than wasting energy and resources

fighting unwinnable political battles, we should instead work on building communities, institutions, and networks of resistance that can outwit, outlast, and eventually overcome the occupation.[2]

I don't agree with Dreher's proposition that we simply drop out of politics, but what can we do when the cultural tide seems to be so opposed to values that matter to families? The cities I used to visit for field trips are no longer pleasant places to explore. In the past you could safely walk through San Francisco, but with homeless addicts now crowding the streets and laws that allow theft up to $900 without prosecution, cities like these feel threatening. Many families are choosing small towns or even rural areas to provide a safer environment for their children.

The Shift

I've been surprised at how fast the world has changed, but the cultural shifts we are facing have been a long time in the making. "Family-friendly" drag shows and gender reassignment surgeries for kids may seem dramatic, and homeless camps in the midst of high rises may be incongruous, but they are just symptoms of a world unmoored from its cultural roots. In *A Christian Manifesto*, published in 1981, Francis Schaeffer wrote,

> The basic problem of the Christians in this country in the last eighty years or so, in regard to society and in regard to government, is that they have seen things in bits and pieces instead of totals.
>
> They have gradually become disturbed over permissiveness, pornography, the public schools, the breakdown of the family, and finally abortion. But they have not seen this as a totality—each thing being a part, a symptom, of a much larger problem. They have failed to see that all of this has come about due to a shift in world view. . . . This shift has been *away from* a world view that was at least vaguely Christian in people's memory (even if they were not individually Christian) toward something completely different.[3]

This post-Christian shift seemed to creep up gradually. Christians and non-Christians often want the same things. We want freedom to raise our families, to make a living, to have a happy life, and there has been a basic code of ethics toward that end. Don't steal, be good parents, don't litter. For the most part, we can agree that life has inherent dignity, that we should help the poor, and that childhood is worth protecting. Some of the new lessons we were learning as a culture in the last decades were good too, such as how to accept our imperfections and to live free from shame. Learning that our bad behavior as adults often stems from childhood trauma is another valuable lesson because it gives hope for change instead of simply deeming people bad or good based on their behavior.

However, I fear we have thrown out the baby of holiness with the bathwater of shame and condemnation. In our desire to be more accepting and affirming as a culture, we've lost some perspective. We are now seeing the results as our culture comes untethered from its Christian moorings and tries to find its way without any shared or timeless values. Suicide and depression are epidemic, twenty-three percent of children are growing up in single-parent homes,[4] and our society has fractured into tribes that argue over healthcare, the environment, sexuality, and education.

> The basic Christian practices that anchored early Christians during the reign of Nero, and Saint Benedict during the Dark Ages, can offer stability and peace to us today.

But there is hope. Even with all these concerning changes, we aren't the first people to live through a dark time in history, and we can look to historic people of faith to help our families stay anchored to biblical truth and connected to each other amid the turbulence. The basic Christian practices that anchored early Christians during the reign of Nero, and Saint Benedict during the Dark Ages, can offer stability and peace to us today. When Saint Benedict was invited into the darkness and depravity of Rome, he chose a different path. He walked away from the world so he could be an instrument of righteousness. He developed basic Christian rules for life that have been in use for more than 1,500 years, helping keep literature, prayer, and order alive. These practices are based on the same biblical principles that guided Jewish families toward the preservation of their culture over thousands of years. Benedict created a school for the service of the Lord and played a part in saving civilization after the fall of Rome.

Sacred Homes

Benedict isn't the only historic Christian who paved a better way in the midst of chaos. In 1900, an Irish woman named Amy Carmichael dedicated her life to rescuing young girls from temple prostitution in India. When she witnessed children being thrown away as sex slaves, she created a sacred home where they could thrive in safety and love.

In the 1930s, a poor pastor's wife and Scandinavian immigrant named Ella Tweten cared for her growing family on the Canadian prairie. As she served the lonely and bereft, her example of love and faithfulness created a legacy of hope in her family and in her community.

In 1950, a Romanian woman named Sabina Wurmbrand lived under the horrifying oppression of Communism. She shared her meager rations with the poor and gathered believers in her home, knowing full well that doing so might mean she would be thrown in prison and tortured. Her service became an international ministry to persecuted Christians.

In 1955, war-torn Europe suffered through the process of rebuilding the broken foundations, and the Schaeffer family created a refuge where people could go to ask the deep questions that consumed their minds. Edith Schaeffer enfolded these seekers into the life of her family, welcoming them around the dinner table and into her daily rhythms. The example she set became a movement throughout a broken world.

In 2023, Christians are outliers, and society is divided into factions based on belief. People in one of the richest countries on earth sleep on the street in makeshift shelters, and violence threatens many. Some would say that we are in a dark age.

But we aren't the first people to live through trying times, and we can learn from what Saint Benedict and the Carmichael, Wurmbrand, Tweten, and Schaeffer families—along with several other historic figures we will study—did to preserve culture and faith in the midst of a chaotic time. They didn't simply adapt to the culture, letting it sweep them along. Instead, each became an island of virtue, a refuge for culture and hope. They created sacred homes for the service of the Lord.

Many of us have been focused merely on raising our children so they can go to college or get a good job, but what if we change our focus to creating an atmosphere that inspires our children toward heroism? What if we create an environment that empowers them to believe they could be the next Amy Carmichael or Saint Patrick or Corrie ten Boom? What if, in addition to having small goals for our children such as passing algebra or writing an essay, we broaden the focus of our homes to ask, "How can we as a family be light in a dark world?"

That's the question this book answers.

Through *Habits for a Sacred Home*, we will step back in time to visit the monastery of Saint Benedict and the homes of the Wurmbrands, Twetens, Grahams, and the Schaeffers. These historic Christians had structures in place that helped prepare people to save the world. These were structures based on the Word of God, and God is calling us also to look to these ancient ways if we want restoration. In Jeremiah 6:16 (NKJV) there is a clear call to a better way: "Thus says the LORD: 'Stand in the ways and see,

And ask for the old paths, where the good way *is,* And walk in it; Then you will find rest for your souls.'" I believe that restoring simple practices such as work, prayer, and stability can help us find rest for our souls and create a refuge for others as well. They can help us educate our children to be world changers, to be light among a crooked and perverse generation.

In *Habits for a Sacred Home,* I identify these practices and give mothers tools for nurturing a life that can make an impact for good in an increasingly chaotic world. I've been a mom for twenty-nine years, and I've seen Christian culture swing wildly between opposite poles of legalism and licentiousness. I've been on that pendulum myself, but I believe there is a better way; we can restore our homes and restore hope for the future by learning from the past. You may have heard the saying that those who don't study history are doomed to repeat it. As I've studied the lives of Christians who have made an impact on the world, I understand that our actions do make a difference. I've been putting these practices into action in my own life, and I want to create a movement of mothers who are nurturing sacred homes that offer hope for restoration. In this book, we will identify nine rules, or habits, Benedict developed in his schools for the service of the Lord: work, stewardship, prayer, order, simplicity, stability, hospitality, community, and balance. We will look at how women such as Amy Carmichael, Sabina Wurmbrand, Edith Schaeffer, and others applied these rhythms to their lives, and we will find practical ways to apply them in our own homes. We don't have to be victims of culture, going wherever the wind blows, nor do we have to languish in fear of the future. God's Word promises salvation for his people—it's only a matter of time.

> Rest in the LORD, and wait patiently for Him;
> Do not fret because of him who prospers in his way,
> Because of the man who brings wicked schemes to pass.
> Cease from anger, and forsake wrath;
> Do not fret—it only causes harm.

For evildoers shall be cut off;
But those who wait on the LORD,
They shall inherit the earth.

Psalm 37:7–9 NKJV

Some of you might be discouraged, feeling you tried to have a sacred home, to have a family who lived by a common, godly rule and it didn't work out. This book is for you as well. I've felt the pain of seeing children make mistakes in their path to adulthood, but mistakes don't define us. Instead of creating a new theology that validates sin and creates destruction in the process, we can stay steady and faithful on the path God has placed us, even if we are the only ones in our family on that path. We can learn how to begin again after we get discouraged or fail. As you will see in the lives of these faithful women, hardships and setbacks are part of life. These women experienced the pain of rebellious children or difficult husbands. They understood the struggles we face on the path of holiness, but those struggles don't define us. What matters is that we get up, dust off the pain and regret, and keep going. Our actions matter, and we can persevere in spite of mistakes and make a difference in the world through our homes.

Even the Chinese philosopher Confucius recognized the power of the home for restoring culture. He said, "The strength of a nation derives from the integrity of the home."[5] I believe that this is true. In a time when the foundations of culture are being rapidly destroyed, we can apply these common practices to our home. I'll even help you create your own customized "family rule," a simple vision and values statement, as you read these chapters. I have provided a template in the appendix, Your Rule of Life, and at the end of each chapter you will identify a few values that can be added to a personalized family rule, a written statement of guiding practices.

You might feel right now that daily faithfulness doesn't really matter, that nobody notices all the dishes you wash, or how you respond kindly in the face of persecution from your teenager, or how you keep on loving your husband through his questioning and doubt. You may feel like the work you are doing in the home, the quiet hidden work of loving your children, and creating a refuge doesn't mean a thing. I think these women, Amy, Ruth, Edith, Mary, Sabina, and others might have felt the same. They were just doing the good works that were right in front of them. They just walked through the next open door, stayed faithful to what God had spoken to them, and they became heroes. They inspired heroism in their people. We can do the same by the power of the Holy Spirit.

We can be those people described in Isaiah 58:12 who "raise up the foundations of many generations," who repair the breach and restore the dwelling places:

> And your ancient ruins shall be rebuilt;
>> you shall raise up the foundations of many generations;
> you shall be called the repairer of the breach,
>> the restorer of streets to dwell in.

We don't know what the future holds, but as we faithfully follow the Word of God, we can create sacred homes, places of joy and hope and life, homes that can push back the darkness until the return of the King.

STUDY GUIDE

Each chapter will end with a few questions to help you evaluate your current "Rule of Life" as well as to create family practices and a culture that reflects your values. The power of the Rule of Saint Benedict was in providing a framework for people in the community to follow that sustained them over the long haul. The same happens in Orthodox Jewish communities. They have clearly defined values that sustain them. As we read each chapter of *Habits for a Sacred Home* and work toward restoring home and culture, we will be defining the practices we want to adopt in our homes by creating a statement that reflects those practices. By the time you have read the whole book, you will have nine clearly defined family values or practice statements to serve as a guideline for your family. These can be plugged into the Your Rule of Life template in the appendix or crafted into a more individualized one of your own making.

Following the Study Guide are suggestions for further reading, a Bible verse to memorize, a prayer, and even a simple recipe to try so that just as the women I highlight gathered their families to break bread together, you can draw your family around the table to discuss these ideas.

With the first chapter, we will ease into the Study Guide by making a simple list of values you have identified for your family. Some examples are:

Honesty	Frugality	Hope
Integrity	Stewardship	Hospitality
Kindness	Mercy	Simplicity
Diligence	Generosity	Excellence

Next, take time to evaluate if your current practices reflect your values. For instance, if generosity is a value but your finances are too overextended to offer help when it's needed, you may need to make some shifts in your spending. Perhaps stewardship is a value, but you are too busy to do basic maintenance on your vehicles. When you identify your values, and the actual practices of your life, you can make adjustments so that your practices are aligned with your values. The following chapters will help you, so don't be discouraged if you realize there is a gap in the values/practices equation.

A VERSE TO MEMORIZE

Stand in the ways and see,
And ask for the old paths, where the good way is,
And walk in it;
Then you will find rest for your souls.

Jeremiah 6:16 NKJV

A PRAYER TO BEGIN

God, thank you for providing redemption from our sins through Jesus Christ. Thank you for making a way to have eternal life with you. You've been so good to us, and we ask that you will intervene for us here on earth as well. Please redeem your people from destruction. Forgive us for the ways we have failed to live by your Word. Help us to look for the ancient ways and obey your commands. Please bring restoration to your people.

2

HABITS OF WORK

EDITH SCHAEFFER

How precious a thing is the human family. Is it not worth some
sacrifice in time, energy, safety, discomfort, work? Does anything
come forth without work?

Edith Schaeffer, *What Is a Family?*

The sun was sinking over the horizon as we gathered near the
bonfire to roast hot dogs. We were tired and dirty, sprinkled
with wood chips after a full day of clearing fallen logs so we
could build a fence for our goats. Even the youngest children had
joined in the work, dragging small branches to the fire, and we
had brought whimsy to the day by using some of the downed
wood to build a miniature log cabin just big enough for us to sit
inside. Of course, we had to shuffle through the tiny doorway on
our hands and knees, but it was worth it to sit in our own shelter.
We wouldn't have survived a South Dakota winter there, but it felt
like an accomplishment.

Our side project brought up questions like "How did Pa and Ma Ingalls build a full log cabin by themselves?" and "How did pioneers survive?" As we talked, we all wondered at the amount of work our ancestors had to tackle just to survive. As we ate toasty hot dogs, we gave thanks that we would sleep in our cozy home for the night instead of bunking down in the cramped and drafty miniature cabin we had built.

We spent many such workdays as we were raising our seven children; our vision of living in the country and growing some of our own food meant that labor was an integral part of our life. While I might wish that I could go back and do some things differently as a mother, I know that the effort of teaching my children how to work, and modeling work as a creative and necessary part of life, was a gift to them and the world. It takes work to save civilization, and it's one of the lessons taught in our home. When we bought a derelict five acres in 2010, the property had been abandoned for a year. The bank had painted over the mouse droppings and put in new carpet, but the smell was still pungent. The previous owner had been plagued with vice, and the result had been barns eaten by starving horses, a home infested with rodents, and fields covered in downed wood. Turning this place into a home was going to take sweat equity, and we were willing to tackle it because we knew that work has the potential to make the world more beautiful.

> When God renews our hearts, we can't help but renew our surroundings. New life in Christ is characterized by regeneration, first in our hearts, and then in every area of our lives.

We began by gutting the kitchen—because no amount of paint was going to cover up the stench of rodent urine—but eventually we renovated every room in the house. Some of the changes were simple, such as painting over the dated volcano rock fireplace in the living room and installing new floors, but other changes involved taking down walls and discovering that the builders had used carpet padding for insulation. No wonder we were so cold! During our six years in that house, we made many small improvements to create order and beauty, and the home became a center of hospitality. Strangers parked their Airstream in our yard and became friends, foreign exchange students spent their summers with our family, and countless worship nights and marriage support groups were held on our patio or in our living room. Our work was part of a rhythm, *ora et labora* ("pray and work," the motto of the Benedictines), and we pushed back the darkness in that home and in that neighborhood through the leading of the Holy Spirit.

We weren't doing anything that extraordinary though—we were just doing what Christian saints through the ages have done as a response of love to God. When God renews our hearts, we can't help but renew our surroundings. New life in Christ is characterized by regeneration, first in our hearts, and then in every area of our lives.

Edith Schaeffer Worked to Save the World

Edith Schaeffer is a prime example of the power of work for regenerating culture. She moved with her family from Pennsylvania to the mountains of Switzerland after World War II, intent on creating a place where people could come with their questions and hear wisdom from the Bible. Creating a place of hospitality while parenting four young children and writing countless books was no calling for the fainthearted, however. Each day she was tasked with feeding groups of people on a meager missionary budget, growing food, caring for children, and providing lodging. I've hosted countless people and I know how much work it takes to wash and change sheets, prepare meals, and clean bathrooms, but Edith cared for people with diligence out of love for God. In her autobiography of their work in Switzerland, Edith writes,

> Sometimes when difficult times are being lived through it seems as though the difficulties are simply too mundane to be the least bit worthwhile. Martyrs being tortured or persecuted for their faith at least sounds dramatic. Having to cook, serve meals to two sittings at times without ever sitting down to eat in between yourself, having constantly to clean up spilled and broken things, to empty mounds of garbage, and to scrub a stove that things have boiled over on, or an oven in which things have spilled over and baked to a black crust is neither dramatic nor glamorous! For the ones who were leading discussions or answering questions or teaching, L'Abri had no set hours which had a beginning and ending time, and so often a sigh of relief, and a relaxing with a cup of tea, has been immediately broken into with the arrival of a new person, or a batch of persons, who needed to be cared for. The Lord was sending people and amazing things were "springing forth", but the prayer answers brought with them the need to be willing to accept all that the answers meant, in the way of work, as well as excitement.[1]

Reading her thoughts on the life they were living brings tears to my eyes. As busy mothers, we often complain about the work of caring for our homes, seek to escape the work, or simply let our families live with chaos instead of putting in the work of making our little world better. Edith didn't shirk the work. Rather, she embraced caring for her family, and expanded that work for the sake of the gospel. She fed strangers over and over again so that the warmth of her hearth would open their hearts to hear of the goodness of God. She hosted fifty people every Sunday for high tea. She prepared rooms for travelers at the drop of a hat. The aim of her work was not only to make her own home more beautiful but to create a ripple of beauty around the world. In a *Christianity Today* article about her family, Os Guinness wrote,

Edith Schaeffer was one of the most remarkable women of her generation, the like of whom we will not see again in our time. I have never met such a great heart of love, and such indomitable faith, tireless prayer, boundless energy, passionate love for life and beauty, lavish hospitality, irrepressible laughter, and seemingly limitless time for people—all in a single person.[2]

Edith diligently served her family and all who entered her doors, and her legacy is still remembered today.

On the other hand, when people avoid work, the opposite happens. In the summer of 2021, businesses were forced to close not only because of a COVID pandemic-related ordinance, but because there were no workers. If you did find an open restaurant or coffee shop, they were often understaffed, as indicated by overflowing garbage cans and long wait times. Fast-food businesses in my state advertised sign-on bonuses and benefits in an effort to attract workers. On car lots, there were no vehicles for sale, as supply chain issues halted new inventory. Maybe some of these changes were needed; after all, how many fast-food restaurants do we really need, and must we upgrade our cars so often? However, breakdowns in service industries and supply chains are certainly indicative of bigger issues. In 2021, business strategists McKinsey & Company warned, "If this labor shortage continues, there will be rising wages, inflation, and supply chain issues in the short term. In the long term, it could halt GDP growth, induce a recession, and cripple the future expansion of sectors dominated by blue-collar and manual workers."[3]

We aren't the first culture to experience upheavals that affect societal norms and comforts. Europe must have been in an even more intense state of chaos in the early years after the Schaeffers arrived in Switzerland. It was just after World War II, and much of the continent was in ruin. Margaret MacMillan wrote in an article for the *Guardian*, "1945 was different, so different that it has been called Year Zero. The capacity for destruction had been so much greater than in the earlier war that much of Europe and Asia lay in ruins. And this time civilians had been the target as much as the military. The figures are hard to grasp: as many as 60 million dead."[4]

For many of us, it is hard to picture what that kind of destruction looks like, and I hope we never have to. But in every culture and time period, after every crisis, it is work that brings restoration. As I write this, swaths of Florida are devastated by a hurricane, but there are workers lined up and ready to restore power, treat the water, and make the area function once more. And remember Saint Benedict, who left the comforts and depravity of Rome, letting it fall while he set himself aside to work, pray, and teach others to do the same. Centuries later, he was honored for his efforts: "In 1964, in view of the work of monks following the Benedictine Rule in the evangelization and civilization of so many European countries in the Middle Ages, Pope Paul VI proclaimed him the patron saint of all Europe."[5]

Work as Art

What motivated Edith Schaeffer and Benedict to work toward transformation? I believe that neither of them set out to save the world, but they were both just being obedient to what God called them to—and yet their individual diligence, centuries apart, impacted the lives of many. There is a closer glimpse of the driving force behind Edith Schaeffer's diligence in her book, *The Hidden Art of Homemaking*. She writes, "There is singing and music which lie in the future—a beauty in the future too—designed, created and prepared by the same Artist whose work we have seen. True enough, all this work of His has been spoiled by sin in the universe, so we cannot fully know what the perfection of the future will be like. But He is the same Artist whose workmanship we have lived with, and enjoyed."[6]

You see, her vision of work was not that it was drudgery or a curse. She saw that God is an artist, and that artists create, which in turn takes work. Consequently, since we are made in his image, we also are made to create. It's a gift. It should leave us in awe that the God who set the stars in the sky and dreamed up the beauty of fruit and flowers created us in his image with the capacity to be creative. And that is what work is: work is creativity. When we clean a bathroom, make a bed, or cook a thousandth meal for our family, we are being creators, we are following God's example. So the first practical step to restoration through work is to embrace work as an opportunity to be creative. If you're longing for joy in your work, this mental shift might be a missing ingredient. When we start to look at the many duties involved in running a home or caring for a family as art, as an opportunity to partner with the Creator to bring order into chaos, it changes everything.

Work Creates Peace

I had a busy summer. My first book, *Mothering by the Book*, had just been released, and I spent many hours recording podcasts or traveling to conferences. Each hour spent away resulted in growing chaos in the functionality of my home. One of my children is still developing good habits, and every time I walked by their bedroom without the time to help them bring order brought a shudder to my heart. Chaos was creeping into my home, which created feelings of confusion and defeat as it grew harder to find things. The more I didn't show love to my home, the more careless my family became. They were doing their best to keep up the good habits, but when there is no leadership or example to follow, chaos quickly ensues. You have to inspect what you expect, and when we fail to consistently train the habits we want our children to display, we can't be upset when their habits reflect the lack of training. When summer ended, it was a great relief to begin methodically working through each room of my house, pulling everything out of drawers and closets and ridding my home of accumulated extras. It brought a feeling of peace and joy to the whole family as I returned my focus to enforcing good habits and daily, life-giving rhythms. As I began to reinforce a healthy routine again and to diligently care for my surroundings, my family members were able to expand their skills as well. It was amazing to see how my renewed focus and leadership created a ripple effect of order and peace in the home.

This is the kind of power you carry in your home as well. The example you set is seen and followed by your children and by those around you. It doesn't happen overnight, but you are setting the tone for what life should be like. When you apply yourself to the work of creating a home and nurturing a family, the people around you notice.

I have the privilege of living in a community of moms who live this out. We gather regularly for book clubs and homeschool co-op classes, but we also have circles of influence that don't overlap. These moms don't all do the same kinds of work, but each of them is creating an inspiring home. One friend cares for many animals on her farm along with homeschooling her four children, and every time I go to her house I'm inspired by something she has done. She has gifts in organization (her pantry is beautiful!). Her children bake amazing chocolate cupcakes, and they raise enough meat to share with other local families. Another dear friend hosts exchange students, birthday parties, and baby showers with beautifully arranged flowers, and her husband brews perfect tea for the many friends who stay with them. Still another manages our homeschool co-op, raises meat, and supports her husband's local government role. Others play instruments, take meals to new moms, and serve in the local church. And one of my first friends in our mountain community does everything in her home with such excellence that she inspires all of us in the community.

These friends have adopted children out of foster care, served the poor, taken mission trips, and loved their neighbors. Each of these women is creative in her own unique way, and diligent, and their work is creating beauty in our community. Their families are known in the gates (they truly are Proverbs 31 women) and this one small town is being restored through their efforts. The community we live in is regenerating; we are pushing back the darkness because the people who live here see work as an opportunity to be creative and resourceful. They don't do everything all the time, though; there are seasons for bigger projects, so if you are in the season of new babies, don't despair. Instead, learn to recognize the joy of work and begin by diligently caring for yourself and your new baby. Start steadfastly loving your own small circle, and that circle of ability and influence will expand.

The opposite happens when the culture begins to be characterized by a lack of diligence. When society looks upon work as punishment, and the need to work as victimization, we see civilization start sputtering to a halt. Instead of work bringing about peace and beauty, systems no longer run smoothly, and filth and confusion ensue from antipathy toward work. What contributes to this apathy and lack of discipline? I think it is natural for us to want to make our surroundings better, so why do some people seem to just not care?

Work Doesn't Equal Victimization

One factor that kills the joy of work is when people start believing they are victims. When people believe that nothing they do matters or that someone is out to get them, that kills initiative. You can see this play out in the lives of people who believe someone else should take care of their needs. You can see it in the lives of people who blame the wealthy and insist they deserve a living wage that isn't tied to contributing to society. And I've even seen it in my own life, during certain seasons when it felt there was just too much work to manage. The unending cycle of laundry and meals and dishes created a sense of hopelessness in my heart. When all my children were small, and my husband worked long hours away from home, the work did seem insurmountable, and I truly felt victimized every time a child got sick and threw up on the bed, or when the baby's diaper leaked, necessitating more laundry loads. It felt like that one extra set of dirty sheets was a tyrant just trying to bury me. During those seasons, I had the choice to either give up and drown in dirty laundry or keep putting one foot in front of the other. I'm a steward of these children, and God's Word says, "It is required in stewards that a man be found faithful" (1 Corinthians 4:2).

I wonder how Edith Schaeffer managed the huge weight of running a home, not just for her own four children, but for countless strangers as well? How did she not grow bitter and feel victimized by the constant demands on her time? Her daughter Susan's book *For the Family's Sake* gives one clue: "When I was very little in America, the Depression was recent enough that many tramps came through the neighborhood looking for a hot meal. How I loved helping my mother set a special tray of good food for the hungry man on the back porch. She never, ever turned anyone away. I grew up hearing that indeed you might be serving an angel 'unawares.'"[7]

So I think the first step in Edith Schaeffer working with joy instead of feeling victimized by labor was to recognize that her work was for the Lord. She acknowledged that any meal she served might potentially be in service to God and his angels (Hebrews 13:2). Each act of love was a gift, not just to her family or her community, but also to God. "And whatever you do, do it heartily, as to the Lord and not to men, knowing that from the Lord you will receive the reward of the inheritance; for you serve the Lord Christ" (Colossians 3:23–24 NKJV). As she served the hobos in her hometown, or the questioning students in the mountains of Switzerland, Edith recognized that her acts of love could pave the way for them to know God. She saw her work as purposeful and important.

This thought has sustained me as well. As I see the way my adult children show hospitality, plant gardens, build furniture, and try new recipes, I'm reminded of how powerful our work is. What we do is transformative. In 1 Thessalonians 4:11–12 (NIV),

Paul urges the people to "make it your ambition to lead a quiet life: You should mind your own business and work with your hands, just as we told you, so that your daily life may win the respect of outsiders and so that you will not be dependent on anybody."

Keep Work in Balance

But work must stay in balance with the practice of rest in order to curb the victim mindset. In the Benedictine tradition, the monks had a daily spread of work, prayer, and study, rather than constant productivity, and in Edith Schaeffer's book about the Ten Commandments, *Ten Things Parents Must Teach Their Children*, she reminds us of the biblical exhortation to take a day of rest. She says, "We need to prepare for the Lord's Day each week in a sincere and very real way, so that we and our children may know something of the keeping of the fourth commandment now, for 'rest and gladness' as well as worship, for God's glory as well as man's good."[8]

Keep Your Priorities in Order

Some of us may be fighting against a tendency toward indolence, leaving dirty dishes in the sink overnight instead of cleaning diligently, leaving babies in wet diapers too long instead of caring for them, or making too many plans for fun instead of choosing needed rest or completing the responsibilities in front of us. But others of us struggle with the opposite problem. We work all day caring for our families, and then stay up late at night prepping for co-op. Or we spend the weekend at a coffeeshop working online instead of taking a day to recharge with our families. Work, though a good thing, is then out of balance, and rest becomes nonexistent.

When we lived on a five-acre farm, I struggled to relax. Everywhere I looked, there were weeds to pull and fruit to process, and it was a juggling act in that season for me to pause and just enjoy my children. It's important to be diligent, but for mothers, one aspect of our work is nurturing our children. Though the days are long, this job has a very finite shelf life; I've experienced the grief as my children became adults and left our home to pursue their own dreams, so we must savor family time now. This means that we need to keep a balance of work and rest, but we also need to create a hierarchy for the work we do. For me, processing the fruit needed to be done, and so did mentoring my children. I had a choice in that moment. I could have them work with me on processing the fruit—they could chop peaches while I heated jars for the jam—or I could let them entertain themselves while I worked. If I chose the latter without taking time to set up boundaries for their activities, I would be making fruit processing a more important work than raising my children. I made that mistake during a season when work felt overwhelming. I placed a higher priority on the physical work of caring for our farm than on the spiritual work of mentoring my children. It was easier to let my children do their own thing rather than train them to help me, or even just to play nearby, and I paid for this lack of prioritizing my work of motherhood with a broken connection with them that took concentrated effort to repair.

It's not that children can never be left on their own. Children do need free time to use their imagination and to problem solve, but in my case, there was a season when I let one kind of work take over everything at the expense of guiding my children. As you examine your own relationship with work and recognize its transformative power, remember to prioritize the *kinds* of work you do. Can you create a hierarchy, so you have some insight into day-to-day work decisions? For instance, God, family, and community might be on a simple list of priorities. But if you are faced with the decision to work on a church event or earn money to buy gas for your car so you can get your kids to school, which option do you choose? Just because the first job is related to church does not mean it is the one that will most glorify God. What about when you have to decide between repainting your living room or homeschooling your kids that day? If your normal routine is putting home improvement projects above homeschooling, you probably should be content with the way your home is and do the work of homeschooling. But if you generally have a good balance of school and home care projects, then there is nothing wrong with teaching your children the life skill of painting instead of hitting the books. It's all about taking time to evaluate our priorities and see if we are living in balance with what God has called us to. Some of us have to work to earn money, and we must put that on the priority list. Some of us have children who need extra care, which also has to be taken into consideration. The objective is that we recognize the transformative power of work while keeping a healthy balance of work and rest. It takes thoughtfulness to decide what work needs to be done now and what can be shelved until later.

If I hadn't been diligent on our farm, my children would have missed some beautiful lessons. Our family celebration days were sweeter because we recognized how precious a day of rest was in the midst of our labors, I just needed to keep it all in balance. If Edith Schaeffer hadn't been diligent to create a place of hospitality and beauty in the mountains of Switzerland, countless students wouldn't have come to know God. and they wouldn't have developed a vision for what a beautiful, godly life could look like. If she hadn't worked to balance her family, home, and authoring of books, we likely wouldn't have her beautiful words, or her daughter Susan's, to guide us in shaping our own families. And your work, whether it's in an office or a field or your home, is transforming the world. Your diligence, your refusal to wait for someone else to pay your mortgage or raise your children or fix your marriage, is making the world more beautiful. You are

> Your work, whether it's in an office or a field or your home, is transforming the world.

changing the world. You might not see the fruit of your labors instantly—the sower doesn't reap the harvest the day after they put the seeds in the ground—but your work is making a difference.

Edith Schaeffer's own son rebelled against the teachings of his parents, but her example of faithfulness and love made such an impact on him that it softened his heart, and he wrote after her passing,

> I'm still thinking of Mom's eternal life in her terms because she showed me the way to that hope through her humane consistency and won. Her example defeated my cynicism.
>
> . . . The day before Mom died my last words to her were "I want you to know your prayers for your family have been answered. I credit every moment of joy to your prayers."
>
> I'll miss her voice. I learned to trust that voice because of the life witness that backed it up. I know I'll hear her voice again. You won Mom. I believe.[9]

As I was speaking at conferences one summer, my youngest daughter sang to the mothers in attendance of the power of their work. She sang to them of the joy and laughter they can look forward to as the fruit of their labors. It was a song written by The Porter's Gate, and it perfectly summarized the importance of your work. *"The houses you labored to build, will finally with laughter and joy be filled."*[10]

———

The world might be broken, and your work unnoticed and unappreciated. Your children might not yet be those who "rise up and call her blessed" (Proverbs 31:28), and you might feel skeptical that they ever will, but still your labor is not in vain. Your faithfulness in putting meals on the table, changing diapers, teaching your children, planting gardens, creating art, and writing heartfelt words is not in vain. The work you are doing is restoring the world.

STUDY GUIDE

What work do you love?

What work do you avoid?

What are your work priorities?

Do you have a good work/rest balance?

Habits of work: Below are a few suggestions for habits you and your family could work toward. Brainstorm your own list to add to these.

Make your bed. Go to bed with a clean sink.

Pick up after yourself. Keep a sabbath.

Load dishes immediately.

Once you have your own list, you can begin to create your family rule by making statements about those habits. By the end of the book, you will have a robust family rule to help guide your daily practices. For example, your statements about work might be:

The _____ family always picks up after themselves.

The _____ family works hard during the week and takes a weekly sabbath.

Or write your own:

_____

_____

When you have decided on your statement about habits of work, you can plug it into the Your Rule of Life template in the appendix.

VERSES TO MEMORIZE

And whatever you do, do it heartily, as to the Lord and not to men, knowing that from the Lord you will receive the reward of the inheritance; for you serve the Lord Christ.

Colossians 3:23–24 NKJV

A PRAYER

God, thank you for the beautiful world you made and the magnificent displays of creativity. Help me to do the work you set before me with joy, knowing that I serve you. Forgive me for the lies I have believed about work and help me to trust that you won't give me more work than I can handle. Amen.

FURTHER READING

L'Abri by Edith Schaeffer
For the Family's Sake by Susan Schaeffer Macaulay

A RECIPE TO TRY

Swiss Zopf Bread

Ingredients

Bread:
- 4 cups flour
- 5 tablespoons softened butter
- ½ tablespoon yeast
- 1½ cups warm milk
- 1 egg
- 1 teaspoon salt

Glaze:
- 1 egg
- 1 tablespoon oil

Instructions

1. Put flour into a large bowl. Cut the butter into small pieces and add to the flour.

2. In a separate bowl, dissolve yeast in the warm milk. Once dissolved, beat 1 egg with the yeast/milk and stir into a flour mixture.

3. Knead dough until it is soft and pliable. It should not be too dry or too sticky. Add the salt and continue to knead for 6–8 minutes.

4. Oil a large bowl and place dough inside, covering it with a towel to rest in a warm place until dough has doubled in size. This should take about 1–2 hours.

5. Using a clean, flat surface, spread some flour to roll dough on. Cut the dough into two equal-sized pieces. Using a rolling pin, roll dough pieces into flat rectangles and then roll them

up lengthwise. This should create two long cylinders of dough of the same length.

6. Place the top two ends together and twist the loaf into one long braid.

7. Place loaf on a baking sheet under a damp cloth to rest for an additional 30 minutes.

8. Preheat the oven to 400 degrees F.

9. While the loaf is resting, combine the egg and oil for glaze.

10. Brush the top with egg/oil mixture, place baking sheet with loaf in the oven, and bake for 40–45 minutes or until golden brown.

11. Remove from the oven and allow to cool.

3

HABITS OF STEWARDSHIP

Mary McLeod Bethune

Faith is the first factor in a life devoted to service. Without it, nothing is possible. With it, nothing is impossible.

—Mary McLeod Bethune, *Building a Better World*

We jumped into the car to head out on our hike, and I noticed the rancid smell as soon as I took the driver's seat. I had tried to regularly remind my kids to grab all their trash and clean up the car when we returned from an outing, but this had been a busy season, which meant more eating in the car, more stuff to unload when we got home, and less energy to put toward cleanup. But I was in a new season and a new year, and one of my goals was to take authority over even the small areas of my life. I wanted to develop the self-discipline to keep my surroundings clean and to teach my youngest two children to do the same. We began by cleaning out all the trash. I reached deep under the passenger seat to grab the bottles I had noticed there, carefully opening the lid to find an unidentifiable and very smelly sludge inside. We vacuumed the floors, peeling up the mats to get underneath, and gave the car a clean slate. Already it smelled better. We started a new habit of removing all trash while filling the car with gas, taking our belongings in when we returned home, and regularly vacuuming the car. The more we worked at basic care of the car, the more we enjoyed our outings, and the more we wanted to take good care of our car. We became good stewards of the gift of a running vehicle, instead of using our car as a dumping ground.

It's easy to see the impact in our homes when we fail to steward our space, and this is true about society as well. In my home state of California, our cities and towns are littered with trash. Homeless camps are visible alongside highways, with salvaged belongings strewn amongst the tents, and trash flowing toward the creeks and highways like a rubbish river. Graffiti and broken glass are commonplace as you walk down city streets, and storekeepers, even in my small town, have to lock up cheap items like razors and toothbrushes because the laws regarding theft are so lax that it seems hopeless to prevent it. One headline claimed that San Francisco's downtown area is more contaminated with drug needles, garbage, and feces than some of the world's poorest slums.

All this decay points to a culture obsessed with nihilism. But we aren't the first society to deal with collective hopelessness and a belief that nothing really matters except personal happiness. The Benedictines were no stranger to nihilism and the destruction that follows. Benedict himself started the monastery after witnessing the decadence and destruction of Rome. They had seen the contrast between a life of peace and the degradation of morals among their fellow Romans. One writer describes it this way: "Many historians note that the final years of the Empire were especially excessive in declining morals and values as witnessed through decreasing safety, promiscuity, lavish overindulgent parties, and violence. During this time the Empire's larger cities were very unsafe because violent crimes were rampant in their streets."[1]

The Contrast

In contrast, the Benedictines set out to steward a life of peace and purpose through clearly defined values, and they took their calling seriously. The brothers were admonished to keep their assigned belongings clean and to treat them with care. They were to avoid wastefulness and extravagance, treating the job of watching over the food, drink, and tools with temperance and faithfulness because they were gifts from God. In Rule 31, regarding the qualifications of the cellarer (the person in charge of the food and goods of the monastery), Benedict writes, "He will regard all utensils and goods of the monastery as sacred goods of the altar, aware that nothing is to be neglected."[2]

So they were to treat even the most mundane items as if they were holy, and I love that change in perspective. In my home, even the cleaning supplies are chosen with care, avoiding those that might be toxic to my family or to the earth, and it's not a big reach to think of each item in my home as consecrated to the Lord. Stewardship is important to God as well. We honor him when we acknowledge what he has given and treat it with care. In Matthew 25, Jesus tells a story about stewardship. A man gives talents (a measure of money) to three of his servants, a different amount to each servant. Two of them invest the money, but the one who receives the least hides it in the ground, afraid of losing it. When the master returns, he is delighted to find that the talents he gave to the first two men had been invested and doubled in value. He tells them, "Well done, good and faithful servant. You have been faithful over a little; I will set you over much. Enter into the joy of your master" (Matthew 25:21, 23).

However, the third servant received quite a different reception. He had buried his one talent in the ground to avoid making a bad investment, the markets going down, or theft. His decision did not please the master. Upon his return, the master chastised the servant for his fearful behavior, saying, "You wicked and slothful servant! You knew that I reap where I have not sown and gather where I scattered no seed? Then you ought to have invested my money with the bankers, and at my coming I should have received what was my own with interest" (Matthew 25:26–27).

God is serious about stewardship. Even mothers at home have a mandate to make "the best use of the time" (Ephesians 5:16), and 1 Peter 4:10 (NIV) is even more explicit: "Each of you should use whatever gift you have received to serve others, as faithful stewards of God's grace in its various forms." We can take this to an extreme, dragging our children out the door over and over to go serve in our church, possibly exhausting our whole family as a result. But there is also the temptation to just stick close to our home and our friends, drinking our "mommy juice" and letting the kids zone out with cartoons while we laugh with our friends about our lack of intentionality. Books are now being written to help the children of these self-absorbed caregivers; *I'm Glad My Mother Died* and *Difficult Mothers* are two examples of many. But rather than giving in to laziness, escapism, or fear, we have the power of the Holy Spirit that enables us to do better and to steward the gifts God has given us.

A Good Steward

Mary McLeod Bethune is a heroic example of taking a mustard seed of faith and turning it into a heroic story. She was born after the Civil War, as the fifteenth child of slaves and the first of their children to be born into freedom. Miraculously, her family had been able to stay together, and not one sibling had been sold away. She grew up in freedom, helping her father plant and harvest cotton and helping her mother wash the neighbor's laundry in exchange for a five-acre piece of land. It took four years of washing to pay for the land, but at last Mary's parents had a place of their own. They built a cabin on that land, trading more work for a mule and a wagon so they could haul their cotton to market. The whole family worked hard in the fields, struggling to earn enough to live on, but they were free, and they were content.

A particular incident marked Mary, however, and gave her a hunger for something more. One day while picking up the laundry to be washed at the home of their former slave owners, she saw a children's book and started to reach for it. Immediately the book's owner said, "Don't you touch that book with your black hands! Don't you know reading is for white folks?"[3]

This birthed a hunger in Mary. Illiteracy among blacks in the South at the end of the Civil War was ninety percent, but Mary was determined to learn. She wanted to prove that reading was for black folks, and especially for her. She prayed to the Lord, "Just give me a chance."[4]

And Mary got her chance. A school opened for black children, and she walked three miles each way so she could learn to read. By her third year in school, she was helping the other students. From the start, Mary took the talents she was given and stewarded them for the betterment of her people. On her days off from school, she spent time teaching younger siblings to read; soon the neighbors, both black and white, came for her help with adding their accounts and getting fair pay from sly merchants. Without math and reading skills, the farmers were being cheated out of their hard-earned money. Sadly, three years after Mary began attending school, the family mule died, forcing Mary to relinquish her time at school to help her father plow the fields.

But God had more opportunities for Mary. A Quaker seamstress in Colorado wrote to a Presbyterian mission school for the children of freedmen, offering to pay tuition for a child they deemed worthy of the honor. They chose Mary. Through the years away from school, whether she was picking cotton or helping her mom iron clothes for her customers, Mary was praying for one more chance to learn. When the news came that she had been selected, she stayed on her knees in the cotton field and thanked God for the opportunity. It was just the beginning. She would go on to finish her education, open a school for girls, and even become an advisor to presidents. One biographical sketch includes this description of just one of her industrious efforts:

> Dr. Bethune famously started the Daytona Literary and Industrial Training Institute for Negro Girls on October 3, 1904, with $1.50, vision, an entrepreneurial mindset, resilience, and faith in God. She created "pencils" from charred wood, ink from elderberries, and mattresses from moss-stuffed corn sacks. . . . In less than two years, the school grew to 250 students.[5]

Mary didn't stop stewarding her talents with the founding of the school. She went on to achieve many other awards for her service to humanity. In an article for the National Women's History Museum, editor Debra Michals highlights more of Mary's accomplishments. In 1936, "President Franklin Roosevelt named her director of Negro Affairs of the National Youth Administration, where she remained until 1944. . . . In 1940, she became vice president of the National Association for the Advancement of Colored Persons (NAACP), a position she held for the rest of her life."[6]

Her tenacity to steward the little she was given created opportunities for African Americans in the midst of racial injustice. She grasped hold of a mustard seed of resources and boldly created mountains of opportunities, one small task at a time. Her daily habits contributed toward the vision she had, and she allowed her love for God and her people to move her toward greatness.

Stewardship is built with the smallest of decisions. Will I pray when I wake up, or look at my phone? Will I read the Bible to my children, or let them watch cartoons all morning? Will I spend my leisure time browsing my favorite stores online or working on a handcraft? None of the options I listed is necessarily bad, but some of them might be more intentional and life-giving in the long run—and it is small daily choices that build a life. Tish Harrison Warren writes in *Liturgy of the Ordinary*,

> We have everyday habits—formative practices—that constitute daily liturgies. By reaching for my smartphone every morning, I had developed a ritual that trained me toward a certain end: entertainment and stimulation via technology. Regardless of my professed worldview or particular Christian subculture, my unexamined daily habit was shaping me into a worshiper of glowing screens.[7]

What are the unexamined daily habits of your life? Are your intentions and your habits in alignment? Do you have intentions? As Christians, we don't have to have the most grandiose dreams. It's okay to have modest intentions, and sometimes it's enough to simply take our cue from a catechism: "Man's chief end is to glorify God, and to enjoy him forever."[8]

To faithfully steward your home, children, marriage, and faith is an admirable and worthy goal. We don't all have to paint masterpieces, invent the next life-saving technology. We don't all have to start schools for the poor, or feed the homeless, but if glorifying God means using the gifts he has given you for his glory, then we need to "do the next thing" with intentionality and love.

As women, we often go to extremes in the area of stewardship. Some women see raising their children as their one thing, but when the children are grown, they shut themselves away from life. They never allowed themselves to dream about the future or to cultivate interests along the way, so they have no grid for exercising stewardship over any area of their life aside from child-rearing. Other women are overly engaged, rushing from church function to work to home, with no margin for stewarding their own health and peace with God. In a sacred home, we can do better. We can spend time with God *and* let the seeds of talents germinate in quiet times with him. We can look at the Scriptures *and* understand what they say about our duties, and we can pace ourselves as we steward the gifts he has given us.

I spent the first twenty-five years of my marriage mainly focused on raising my children and loving my husband. As a family, we went on short-term mission trips, lived in Mexico for a season and helped an orphanage, and after we returned home, we spent years facilitating local marriage ministry. We felt that using the gifts God gave us for a bigger purpose than just our own family fun was a way we could inspire our children to use their talents wisely. My main focus was my children, but even in child-rearing, I tried to steward the task. I researched the best ways to feed, educate, and parent them. I spent time sharing nature with them and reading beautiful stories aloud. I looked at mothering my children as a calling from God, and I gave it my all. A faulty, messy all at times, but I get an A for effort.

> In a sacred home, we can spend time with God *and* let the seeds of talents germinate in quiet times with him, look at the Scriptures *and* understand what they say about our duties, pace ourselves as we steward the gifts he has given us.

The time I spent stewarding my calling as a mother grew beyond my children. As my passion for educating them well and understanding their development grew, it led to writing homeschool curriculum, and my Peaceful Press resources have now been used by thousands of families to bring more peace and connection to their homes. The popularity of my curriculum led to speaking, podcasting, and writing books. It led to communities of mothers being empowered to educate their children. Stewarding the children God gave me opened other opportunities to use my gifts for him. I take no opportunity for granted, and it's an honor to serve my Lord. There were moments when I was tempted to give up on mothering or homeschooling or my business, but I'm too in love with Jesus to stop serving him.

Some of you might feel that you have nothing to steward or that you don't have any special talents. I understand. When I was a very young mother, my pre-motherhood jobs were uninspiring, and my family of origin had few connections and fragile finances. I wasn't starting out with much. However, compared with Mary McLeod Bethune, I was privileged. She had no money, a few years of schooling, and impoverished parents. But with the little spark she had, she nurtured a roaring fire of opportunity for her people. A little bit of education led to her starting a school. A little bit of concern for the sick led to her starting a hospital. She advocated for her community her entire life, turning whatever talents she had into a gold mine.

And stewardship can be applied to so many areas of our lives.

Physical health: Simple practices such as drinking a morning cup of hot water before flooding your system with coffee can help your body detox. Caring for your teeth (and teaching your children to care for theirs), eating fresh vegetables and fruit, avoiding chemicals, and getting daily exercise help us have the health and energy needed to participate with God in restoring culture. Getting outside every day helps your body produce beneficial vitamin D and serotonin. Getting enough sleep at night helps us reset so we can think clearly and have patience with our families. If we can't even steward our own health, if we stay up too late every night, overdo it on alcohol every weekend, neglect exercise, and don't eat healthfully, we will be sabotaging restoration before we even get started.

Relationship with God: Our quiet time with God must be stewarded. In the busy years with small children, it can feel impossible to pray and read our Bibles, but God has promised to reward those who diligently seek him. We can play an audio Bible while we are caring for an infant, or pray while we make breakfast, but we need God's direction and help as we navigate these turbulent times. The

Benedictines gathered multiple times each day for prayer, they studied his Word, and they made pursuit of him the principal thing. We might think we don't have the margin to set apart time with God; however, if we can find time to scroll our phones but can't find time to pray, read our Bible, or even just sit and enjoy his presence, then we might not be very self-aware. If we say we love him, we need to find time to be with him. We must create daily rhythms that incorporate time with him into our day. You can read the Bible at the breakfast table with the children in the morning, recite the Lord's Prayer as they go to bed, and take some time as you wake up or go to sleep to just breathe and think about how much he loves you. These little prompts will start to make a difference in every area of your life.

Children: One contributor to the problems we face in culture is that Christian families have not stewarded their children well. We are told what our duty is in Deuteronomy 6:6–7: "And these words that I command you today shall be on your heart. You shall teach them diligently to your children, and shall talk of them when you sit in your house, and when you walk by the way, and when you lie down, and when you rise."

The most basic command of stewardship from God is that we would hear his instructions and teach them to our children. So instead of passively handing our children over to a failing system, let's find creative ways to lift up the Bible at home and talk regularly about what God loves. A return to basic Christian norms of civility is essential to restoration, and our children need to be taught simple principles such as don't steal, don't covet, and don't commit adultery. We can't force other people to steward the character of their children, but we can teach ours to be salt and light in the world. We can't stop other people from raising kids who steal, but we can teach ours to work for what they want and live within their means. We can't stop people from raising children who think it's okay to express hate or physically vandalize businesses, but we can teach ours to have self-control. We can take the time to teach ours to obey God and trust that he will watch over his people. As we reignite practices in our families that convey our values, we will see a change. These practices might be simply reiterating your family values around the dinner table, playing games instead of watching movies that aren't uplifting, or taking a family walk instead of letting your children scatter to their rooms. Stewarding our children means simply doing our best to pass on biblical wisdom and a knowledge of how much God loves them, instead of allowing the values of the world to be the loudest voice.

Home: Our homes can be little monasteries, a refuge from the chaos of the world, but it takes nurture to build a peaceful home. Usually, the little people in our homes make the messes, but sometimes it is our own bad habits that do. When we get in the habit of going to bed with a clean kitchen, hanging up our clothes after we wear them, and teaching our children to pick up after themselves as well, we are nurturing tidy spaces where company is comfortable to gather. It might take time to get these habits in place, and some of our children will be more drawn to these habits than others, but eventually your children will make their own beds and clean their own rooms. They may even help with the meals and clean up the rest of the house instead of merely making messes, as we model and teach stewardship of our homes.

Finances: Just as the righteous servants took the talents they were given and used them for good, we can take the money we have and use it wisely. We often create stress and pressure for ourselves by buying things to augment a frail identity, instead of making financial decisions wisely. Perhaps Mary McLeod Bethune was able to do so much with so little because her purpose was more important than her image. She wasn't trying to get people to like her, she was trying to help people live free, and she used money toward that end. Maybe the most helpful thing you can do in stewarding your finances is to define what is important to you. When you know that, it's easy to make food at home instead of eating out because you are saving to buy a home where your children can enjoy nature. Or maybe you buy your clothes at a thrift store because you don't want to support clothing companies that treat their garment makers poorly. Knowing your values and purpose can help you steward your finances.

Time: Our time is a finite gift; so many of us are losing our ability to be creative because we spend every leisure moment looking at *others'* creativity on social media. Instead of letting our phones dictate how our time is spent, we must create a rhythm for our day with first things first. Develop a morning routine that allows time for Scripture, prayer, and exercise. Create a school rhythm with time for painting or looking at art. Work on a rhythm for money-earning activities that keeps phone use in its proper place. Restoration requires inspiration. If Saint Benedict hadn't been cultivating the mental space to listen to God, he wouldn't have had the inspiration to create a rule for saving civilization. If Mary McLeod Bethune hadn't been cultivating mental space to dream about how life could be better for her and her people, she wouldn't have gone to the trouble of starting a school. Just imagine the transformational power of your family when you have the gift of time to step back and reflect. So take some time as you read this book to log your time, writing down how you spend your hours over the course of a week. Being intentional about tracking what you do with the gift of time will help you see if you are stewarding your time well.

I was away from my home for several months one year, living in a temporary Airbnb while my husband did a ministry program. My oldest daughter, a twenty-something adult, cared for our home while we were gone, relishing the peace and quiet. During this time, she planted winter greens, butchered a goat, stacked wood, kept the house clean, and maintained our own Airbnb while working and researching. She is a faithful steward. I knew that I could trust her to take the little that she presided over and make it more beautiful and productive than it was when we left. When my Lord returns, I want him to be able to say the same about me. I want him to find me ready, with my lamp full and polished. I want him to find me ready for the wedding, because of love. "And I heard, as it were, the voice of a great multitude, as the sound of many waters and as the sound of mighty thunderings, saying, 'Alleluia! For the Lord God Omnipotent reigns! Let us be glad and rejoice and give Him glory, for the marriage of the Lamb has come, and His wife has made herself ready'" (Revelation 19:6). Love for God and for her people motivated Mary McLeod Bethune to create schools and hospitals so they could be educated and well. Love can help you steward the talents in your hands as well, and this loving stewardship can bring restoration to the world around us.

STUDY GUIDE

How was stewardship modeled in your family of origin?

How have you stewarded your resources?

What areas do you steward well?

What areas could you work on?

Habits of stewardship: These are a few suggested habits, but you can add your own and then fill in the blanks below with a few to work on.

Eat healthfully

Exercise

Pray

Read the Bible to yourself
and your children

Define your values

Think before you spend

Care for your belongings

Allow margin in your
schedule

Track your time

What habit will you adopt in your family? For example, your statements about stewardship might be:

The _____ family exercises every day.

The _____ family cares for our belongings.

Or write your own here:

_____

_____

When you have decided on your statement about habits of stewardship, you can plug it into the Your Rule of Life template in the appendix.

⸺ A VERSE TO MEMORIZE ⸺

Moreover, it is required of stewards that they be found faithful.

1 Corinthians 4:2

⸺ A PRAYER ⸺

Dear God, thank you for all the gifts you have given me. Forgive me for the ways that I have neglected to steward them. Give me the strength to steward each day as a gift and to keep my heart turned toward you in love.

FURTHER READING

Mary McLeod Bethune by Emma Gelders Sterne
Atomic Habits by James Clear
The Lifegiving Home by Sally Clarkson

A RECIPE TO TRY

Groundnut Stew

2 pounds chicken thighs
1 large onion, chopped
6 cloves crushed garlic
1 3-inch piece of ginger, peeled and minced
1 small poblano chile, chopped
4 small sweet potatoes, peeled and cut into small chunks
1 15-ounce can of crushed tomatoes
1 quart chicken stock
½ cup peanut butter
1 teaspoon ground coriander
1 teaspoon ground cumin
salt to taste
black pepper to taste
¼ to ½ cup chopped cilantro

PREP: 20 minutes COOK: 40 minutes TOTAL: 60 minutes

1. In a heavy Dutch oven or other covered pan, brown chicken, onion, garlic, and ginger in oil until onions are translucent.

2. Add remaining ingredients, stirring until well combined.

3. Bring to a boil and then reduce heat and simmer covered for 45–60 minutes or until chicken is cooked and flavors are combined.

Makes 6 servings.

4

HABITS OF PRAYER

Amy Carmichael

I do not think anything worth having in the spiritual world is easily attained. There is no shortcut to holiness. But there can be a true, humble, loving choice of the soul, and that choice, becoming a habit, will lead it into peace.

Amy Carmichael, *Edges of His Ways*

My 73-year-old mother and I carefully stepped through the field of rocks, checking our footing before we moved on to the next boulder. Huge stones had fallen here and shaped a landscape that looked like something you would imagine in a *Lord of the Rings* movie. It was green with slick moss, and though it looked beautiful, it was treacherous to walk through. What was even more treacherous was the climb my daughter was attempting up the sheer face of the cliff just a hundred feet in front of where I stood watching. We had all driven to the trailhead together, but

I was slowly navigating the slippery rocks with my aging parents while my children raced ahead to start the climb.

I paused in my careful navigation to watch my daughter traverse the rock face while my heart beat rapidly. She was sixty feet above the ground, and I knew that she was setting up the climb for her less experienced younger sister, which made me even more scared. The sun was setting, and fear gripped me as I thought of her and her sister navigating the rock face in the evening dusk and then driving out through the deeply pitted road, even while wondering how I was going to help my elderly mom and dad on the return walk through the boulders. I was accustomed to the battle of overcoming fear, but a stressful Christmas season with hospital visits, a relationship crisis, and then watching my daughters scale the rock face created a whirlwind of anxiety in that moment. With so much out of my control, all I could do was breathe deeply and pray.

Desperate Prayers

The last few years have taught me to pray in ways I've never prayed before. I've always talked to God; even as a young child, I can remember crying out to God when I felt alone or afraid. But being a mother created a paradigm where the task in front of me was greater than my strength, and prayer was as necessary as air. When my children were young, my prayers were simple: "God, please let this child sleep through the night," "Please, please let them make it to the potty," and, "Please help them stop coughing and go to sleep!" The seasons of early motherhood are so full of physical demands, and the endless rounds of birth, sleepless nights, potty training, and childhood illnesses require prayer to sustain us. But mothering adult and teen children requires a whole new level of prayer. Suddenly, we can't just tell our children to do something and expect them to obey. We can't endlessly direct them. They are out of our home, or on their way out, and all we can do is pray that our teaching will stick, or that God will teach them what we didn't. This is where prayer becomes food to us, and where we see how big our faith in God really is.

I've been through a few tough seasons with adult children, and seasons when I couldn't check in on them. One son went to a Bible program on the Mediterranean island of Cyprus. The school didn't allow cell phone use at all, and the students were only allowed calls on Sunday. I couldn't check his location or text him to see how he was doing. The only contact we had were those short calls on Sunday afternoons and the letters we sent back and forth. During this season, I learned to pray in a different way than I ever had before. There was no daily reassurance that my son was safe and happy, and all I could do was commit his life into the hands of God. My prayers were a lifeline, and the God who I called on in my distress of having children far away was the source of my peace.

And then there is my rock-climbing daughter. Dragging a length of rope behind her, she clips herself onto small pins in the face of a cliff as she ascends hundreds of feet in the air. When she's climbing, I can't reach her to see if she's safe, and it's often a long day with no news, until I finally get a call that she's on her way home. During one of her climbing adventures, day turned to night and there was still no word. My anxiety grew, and I had to work to stay calm using strategies like taking my thoughts captive and staying present. My imagination was my enemy in these moments; it was much easier to imagine her in a heap at the bottom of the cliff than cuddled safely into a hammock in the rocks. I was finally able to get a call through to her, only to discover that at 11 p.m., when dark had fallen solidly over Yosemite Valley, she still faced one more cliff face and a long hike back to the car.

We made it through that long night, God brought her home safely, and prayer was the means of keeping my mind and spirit calm as I waited for her return. I've had other seasons when I could text my children all I wanted but needed to learn to let them go a little, to let the Holy Spirit speak to them instead of trying to tell them all the tips that I had for better relationships and a happy life. I wanted to make sure I didn't miss any instructions, that I told them everything they needed to know for life and godliness, but sometimes our words are too much for a child who is trying to become self-governing. Sometimes we need to give them space to make their own mistakes and to learn to rely on God for wisdom instead of trying to be the Holy Spirit for them.

It's been a hard transition for me, because it feels much easier to physically direct my children than to wait on God to direct them. Sometimes I wish I could go back to the simplicity of bedtimes and learning to be consistent with chores, the days of diapers and breastfeeding when all my children were safe within our four walls. I wish I could go back to when all seven of them were with me every day, gathered for our morning time, or working in the garden together. I loved that season, but I didn't realize how much easier it was to parent toddlers than to parent adults.

Now we are praying our way through adult struggles with difficult work environments, or learning to manage life without escaping to video games or social media (I'm still working on this), or trying to maintain healthy relationships with a spouse. The problems adult children face are so much more intense and the consequences greater when mistakes are made. Also, the weapons of prayer we wield to navigate these problems often can seem so passive. How can I really affect change in the world simply by praying, when what I want to do is go rescue my children? How can prayer be effective when it seems like physical action is needed? And why is prayer important anyway?

Jesus says in Luke 21:36 (KJV), "Watch ye therefore, and pray always, that ye may be accepted worthy to escape all these things that shall come to pass, and to stand before the Son of man." We are commanded to pray, even to pray without ceasing, because while we may feel that we can maintain control over our destiny and our family, the reality is that control is just an illusion. We might think we can bring restoration on our own, but our hope lies not in our own works but in the love and goodness of God. Prayer is a way of realigning our minds with that truth, recognizing that God is on the throne and we are not. And prayer is an important part of saving the world, of restoring culture.

The Benedictines, in their own pursuit of restoration, understood this and made prayer a regular practice, meeting several times a day to acknowledge the lordship of Christ. And while the recommendation for prayer in the Benedictine tradition was that they be short, the reality is that the Psalms they were reciting seven times each day were a prayer, and a means of fixing their minds on the reality of God. Most of them are the desperate prayers of David, a man after God's own heart, full of declarations that God is trustworthy and a refuge for the oppressed. Their diligence in meditating on the Psalms—on the truth that God is with us, that he will never forsake us, that he is a refuge to the oppressed—became a bigger reality than the circumstance they feared. Their minds were fixed on a higher plane, which helped them "keep calm and carry on" even when civilization was falling right outside their front door. Doing good works came after knowing the reality of God through his word, and they had faith that God would accomplish his purpose because they relied on his Word. In fact, they recited the full content of the Psalms each week, Saint Benedict himself cautioning that "monks who in a week's time say less than the full psalter with the customary canticles betray extreme indolence and lack of devotion in their service."[1]

> We might think we can bring restoration on our own, but our hope lies not in our own works but in the love and goodness of God. Prayer is a way of realigning our minds with that truth, recognizing that God is on the throne and we are not.

Even with my dedication to daily Scripture reading, the truth is that my thoughts are much more formed by my attention to social media, to the daily comings and goings of my children, and to the news of the world. My time each day is absorbed by homeschooling, homemaking, and online work so that the effect of my Scripture reading becomes engulfed by the cares of the world. Yes, action is an essential part of the Christian walk; we have to care for our families, but we must also start with prayer so we can care for them with clarity and peace. In fact, caring for children can be in itself a spiritual discipline. In his book *Domestic Monastery*, Ronald Rolheiser writes, "If you are home alone with small children whose needs give you little uninterrupted time, then you don't need an hour of private prayer daily. Raising small children, if it is done with love and generosity, will do for you exactly what private prayer does."[2]

The Praying Amma

Another mom understood this striving for quiet time in the midst of caring for a household of many. Amy Carmichael was born in Ireland in 1867, the oldest of seven children. As a teen, she attended boarding schools until her father died when she was eighteen. During these years, she made the decision to leave her loved ones and become a missionary, first setting her sights on China. However, God had other plans for her destination. A missionary board decided that her health wasn't sufficient for the China missionary organization, so after a brief stint in Japan, she went to India, where she spent the rest of her life rescuing young girls from temple prostitution. While caring for the unwanted and abused, she wrote forty books full of loving encouragement to consecrate our lives to the One who is worthy. Amy's words have given me courage when my own faith was small.

When she first arrived in India, Amy was doing evangelistic work, traveling from village to village sharing the gospel. One little girl was getting water when she overheard the story of Jesus. Preena was a seven-year-old temple prostitute, given to the Hindu priests to use and abuse. Ben Sansburn describes this poignant moment that changed the trajectory of Amy's ministry:

> Preena's arrival brought Amy face to face with the dark reality of child sex trafficking. Amy had heard whispers of it, but suddenly it was standing in black and white right in front of her. And the more she began to ask questions, the darker and more horrible that reality became. Amy knew that God was calling her to do something about it.[3]

Amy became known as *Amma*, a Hindi word for mother, to the girls she rescued from temple prostitution; she stretched herself far beyond human strength to love these rejected daughters, and prayer was an essential part of her ministry. She knew the danger these girls were in, and yet it wasn't always within her power to immediately rescue them from their degrading circumstances. Then, even when it was possible, rescue involved danger because the temple priests hated her for interfering in their nefarious work. In her book *Things as They Are*, Amy writes of the desperate interventions they took on behalf of these girls.

> The week passed, and every day we prayed for that little one. Then when the time came, we went. Hope and fear alternated within us. One felt sick with dread lest anything had happened to break the mother's word, and yet one hoped. The house door was open. The people in the street smiled as we stopped our bandy, got out, and went in. I remembered their smiles afterwards, and understood. The mother was there: . . . on the floor asleep, *drugged*, lay the child with her little arms stretched out. The mother's eyes were hard.[4]

Amy and her helpers had tried to rescue this child from being sold as a slave to the temple, but the mother broke her promise and prevented the rescue. Instead of living the innocent life that children deserve, this child was to be trafficked for the pleasure of the depraved. She wasn't the first child Amy was to pray for, nor was she the last. In her lifetime, Amy Carmichael was able to rescue 1,000 girls from temple prostitution, but that number represents many more who were lost to her. It represents many prayers she threw up to God in hopes that he would answer and save these children.

Mothers Understand

We mothers understand this desperation. We love our children and want the best for them, but sometimes we are just throwing our prayers up to God and hoping that he will save. We don't own our children, we can't control their lives, and we must rely on God to move them. Some of you have seen your bright-eyed children who were once full of innocence embrace a lifestyle of depravity. Some of you have seen your beautiful babies reject the God you love. Some of you are simply suffering through childhood illness and disability, thankful that your children are close and yet desperate for freedom from suffering. Life is full of hardship, and we can't control everything that happens to us. Still, we have a God who is in control and who is good. When we make prayer (especially Scripture-informed prayer) a part of our daily routine, we can find rest for our souls and hope for the weary. Prayer is powerful. The Word of God says, "The prayer of a righteous person has great power as it is working. Elijah was a man with a nature like ours, and he prayed fervently that it might not rain, and for three years and six months it did not rain on the earth. Then he prayed again, and heaven gave rain, and the earth bore its fruit" (James 5:16–18).

Amy had the option to sideline prayer in favor of active work such as feeding children or evangelism, but she understood the importance of time spent with God. In order to have the power to obey God and to bring restoration to a culture that was decaying in sin, she needed to meet with the Source of that power. She wrote,

The fight to which we have been called is not an easy fight. We are touching the very center of the devil's power and kingdom, and he hates us intensely and fights hard against us. We have no chance of winning in this fight unless we are disciplined soldiers, utterly out and out uncompromising, and men and women of prayer. So first, give much time to quietness. We have to get our help for the most part direct from our God. We are here to help, not to be helped and we must each one of us learn to walk with God alone and feed on His word so as to be nourished. Don't only read and pray; listen. And don't evade the slightest whisper of guidance that comes. God make you very sensitive, and very obedient.[5]

The Work of Warriors

We are called to a similar fight. The work of restoration, of rearing children who love God and who trust in his Word is not an easy one. The work of continuing to pursue God's best for our families even after our children are grown is hard. The work of putting down our phones and being quiet with God, of opening our doors and showing hospitality to a stranger, or of growing a garden in the midst of chaos and war is the work of warriors. We cannot partake in this work without prayer. We are pushing back against darkness; prayer is our best weapon. And we can pray with hope. Even amid the battle, when it feels like all is lost, even when we are walking through what feels like the destruction of our family, or the dreams we had of our family, still we can have hope. Amy Carmichael writes in *Edges of His Ways*, a devotional collection,

> Sometimes it is a help to remember that we are not the only people to be tempted to be cast down. "And if I be cast down, they that trouble me will rejoice at it" (Ps. 13:4) is as true now as it ever was. But look at the words that follow. "My trust is in Thy mercy; and my heart is joyful in Thy salvation. I will sing of the Lord, because He has dealt so lovingly with me: yea I will praise the Name of the Lord Most Highest." (13:5–6 PVB). *That* is where we were meant to live, and where we can live we will live. There is no provision in

the whole Bible for a despondent Christian. "Thanks be unto God, which always causeth us to triumph in Christ" (2 Cor. 2:14)—that is the word for us all.[6]

At the time I read those words, I was struggling with the deepest despond. One of my children was in a painful season, facing a job loss and relationship breakdown, which culminated in physical distress and sickness. My heart was broken as I watched him navigate these circumstances, and I was tempted to lose hope. My dad came to me one day and said, "You are the cheerleader of this operation, and if you are down, everyone is down."

His words shook me out of my funk. It was the holidays, after all, and I didn't want the rest of my children to feel hopeless and discouraged as they watched my husband and me navigate this distressing season. I wanted them to remember that I put on a smile and started singing in the midst of my anguish. I wanted my children to see that my faith in God was bigger than the circumstances, and the only way I could get there was through prayer.

Maybe you are feeling the same stress and anguish. Perhaps you are in your own relationship crisis or dealing with a child who is struggling. We have a refuge in God, and prayer is the way to access that sense of refuge and peace. For Amy Carmichael, daily prayer was essential, and for the Benedictines, the pursuit of God and the restoration that comes from life with God required a daily practice of accessing the peace of God through the Psalms and through prayer.

A Plan for Prayer

Busy mothers need their own handbook for prayer. We often don't have the mental space to come up with a plan, so here are a few possible ways to make prayer a priority in your home.

- **Wake with prayer**—As you wake up in the morning, simply thank God for the day and for breath. Give him your worries, your plans—offer it all to him as you start your day. Say, "God, I give you everyone and everything" as a way of putting your loved ones in his hands.

- **Recite the Psalms**—Read a new psalm every day, or work on the same one for a week. Print it out and put it on the bathroom mirror, on your closet door, or anywhere you pause during your day. The Benedictines recited all 150 psalms each week, but you can start with just one. As you declare the words of the Psalms out loud, you will begin to experience more peace.

- **Practice Lectio Divina**—Latin for "divine reading," this is simply a way of meditating on Scripture. Read a short portion of Scripture, meditate on it, pray the words, and then contemplate God's love for you through that passage.

- **Practice breath prayer**—Navy Seals practice *box breathing* when they are in a tense situation. This is simply inhaling for four counts, holding for four counts, exhaling for four counts, and then holding again for four counts. This helps the nervous system and calms the mind. You can add a prayer to this box breathing. Inhale while thinking the word Jesus, exhale while whispering, "Have mercy on me." You can use a variety of words, Scripture, or historic prayers, to complete the breathing series, but the simple idea is to breathe deeply while meditating on God's love for us.

- **Create a prayer rhythm**—At Dohnavur Fellowship, where Amy Carmichael rescued children, they had set daily and weekly times for prayer. The Benedictines also paused seven times a day for prayer. We are called to pray without ceasing, and yet it can be easy to forget prayer altogether in the busyness of our day, or to only pray when things are desperate. To create a simple prayer rhythm, you can set a few alarms on your phone as a call to prayer. It might just be morning and evening prayers, or you could add a noontime prayer, but making prayer a daily rhythm will infuse you with the peace of God.

- **Encourage family prayer time**—In our home, we often simply pray the Lord's Prayer at the end of the day, declaring forgiveness, and the holiness of God with all who are inside our four walls. It's a simple way to align our family with the truth of God's goodness and presence. We also have morning prayers, praying oldest to youngest, reciting Scripture or the Apostle's Creed so that we start our school day acknowledging God as Lord.

- **Make prayer a conversation**—Talk to God throughout your day, inviting His wisdom into even the smallest of moments. Tyler Staton writes in *Praying Like Monks, Living Like Fools*, "Prayer is as casual as small talk. Asking is the experience of prayer at its most relational."[7]

  When we make prayer a conversation, expressing our feelings, needs, and love throughout the day, we are cultivating a relationship with God. If we are to partner with him for restoration in our homes and communities, we need to spend time with him, and this comes as we cultivate intimacy through conversational prayer.

- **Engage in listening prayer**—Many of us are so scared of making a wrong assumption about what God is saying that we don't even try to listen. However, the path to restoration involves many small decisions with big consequences. Do we stay in our hometown or move to a new state? Do we stand up for what we believe and possibly lose our job? Do we homeschool or send our kids to the local school? Do we go to this church or that one? We are faced with myriad questions each day. And while we have the written Word to direct our steps and to teach us how God speaks, and ultimately to confirm or deny what we think we are hearing, we need to practice the hearing as well. All throughout the Bible, the great men and women of God listened to the messenger and obeyed. Moses listened to God and led his people to freedom. Elijah listened to God, and the false prophets were destroyed. Mary listened to God and bore a son named Jesus. God is the same yesterday, today, and forever, and we need to cultivate a quiet heart so we will know his voice and obey it.

- **Sing your prayers**—During hard seasons, my prayers become desperate pleas, muddled with fear, and peace feels hard to come by. But when I start singing, my body relaxes, and I can sense the goodness of God again. Many of the worship songs we sing, whether old hymns such as "O Come, O Come, Emmanuel" or modern worship choruses like "Jesus, You're Beautiful," were written as prayers. These prayers were penned either to honor God or to plead with him, but with all the love and desperation of humans who are fully aware that while we need restoration, it can only come through the grace of God.

While I was writing this chapter, I was singing for peace and perspective, breathing my prayers, declaring Scripture, and praying together with my family. I was pushing toward the peace of God and breakthrough for my children with everything in me. As Eugene Peterson wrote, "Prayer is the secret work that develops a life that is thoroughly authentic and deeply human."[8]

We can trust that God will carry out the restoration we need in our family and our community. Things may look bleak, and after doing all you thought possible to effect change, there may still be a great chasm between your hopes for the world and the reality of it, but God is always working things out for our good and his glory. Amy Carmichael wrote these words about trusting God's timing,

Sometimes things are allowed to happen so that the quiet power of our Lord to arrange and rearrange events according to his purpose may be shown. The priests did not want Him to be arrested before the feast was over, but He had planned otherwise. "After two days," He said to His disciples, "the Passover cometh and the Son of Man is delivered to be crucified." And so it was. He, not the Priests, decided the order of events. Even so, all through the confusions of life, the quiet purpose of the Lord is fulfilled and nothing can upset it.[9]

His purpose will be fulfilled. His kingdom will come. Nothing can stop the restoration that is coming; as we pray, we are crying out for his kingdom to come, for his will to be done, and for the will to wait quietly for his perfect timing of the salvation we need.

For Our Children

Father, hear us, we are praying,
Hear the words our hearts are saying;
We are praying for our children.

Keep them from the powers of evil,
From the secret, hidden peril;
Father, hear us for our children.

From the whirlpool that would suck them,
From the treacherous quicksand, pluck them;
Father, hear us for our children.

From the worldling's hollow gladness,
From the sting of faithless sadness,
Father, Father, keep our children.

Through life's troubled waters steer them;
Through life's bitter battle cheer them;
Father, Father, be Thou near them.

Read the language of our longing,
Read the wordless pleadings thronging,
Holy Father, for our children.

And wherever they may bide,
Lead them Home at eventide.

Amy Carmichael[10]

STUDY GUIDE

How have you experienced prayer?

When do you feel closest to God?

Remember a time when you felt close to God. Thank him for being near.

Habits of Prayer: Which of these habits will you add to your family rule?

Morning prayer

Evening prayer

Breath prayer

Praying Scripture

Lectio Divina

Listening prayer

Singing Scripture or hymns
as prayers

What rule will your family adopt regarding prayer?

For example, the _____ family prays together every morning and evening.

The _____ family prays Scripture before meals.

Or write your own here:

_____

_____

When you have decided on your statement about habits of prayer, you can plug it into the Your Rule of Life template in the appendix.

——— VERSES TO MEMORIZE ———

Do not be anxious about anything, but in everything by prayer and supplication with thanksgiving let your requests be made known to God. And the peace of God, which surpasses all understanding, will guard your hearts and your minds in Christ Jesus.

Philippians 4:6–7

——— A PRAYER ———

God, thank you for hearing our prayers. Thank you that we can come to you when we feel anxious. Forgive me for the times I have gone to other things for comfort instead of seeking you. Help me to truly trust that you are good and that you are working things out for my good and your glory. Help me to rest in your love for me and my family. Amen

——— FURTHER READING ———

Edges of His Ways by Amy Carmichael
Candles in the Dark by Amy Carmichael
Praying Like Monks, Living Like Fools by Tyler Staton

A RECIPE TO TRY

Flatbread

3 cups flour
1 teaspoon dried oregano
or basil

1 teaspoon salt
3 tablespoons olive oil
1½ cups water

PREP: 20 minutes COOK: 10 minutes TOTAL: 30 minutes

1. Process ingredients in a food processor until a loose dough is formed.

2. Transfer dough to a floured surface and knead for 5 minutes.

3. Place in an oiled bowl and rest for 20 minutes.

4. Divide dough into 12 pieces and roll each piece into a flat circle.

5. Lightly oil a heavy skillet and cook each about 2 minutes for each side.

6. Serve warm.

5

HABITS OF ORDER

Elisabeth Elliot

Any "soldier," any candidate for Christian discipline, ought daily to report to his commanding officer for duty. At your service, Lord.

Elisabeth Elliot, *Joyful Surrender*

When my first five children were all very young, we read *The Story about Ping* aloud. In this story of a family of ducks and their fishing boat on the Yangtze River, the master would give a sing-song call, and each duck would race to the boat to avoid being left behind. It was just a cute story to us until one day at a barbecue we saw a mom ring a bell—and her children all came running! We were inspired. How much easier and more pleasant would it be to simply whistle or ring a bell and get your children to come? No more would we have to call out every single name when it was morning or dinner time; now we could gather the troops quickly. We decided to try this method. Our whistle was our version of the master's call in *Ping*, and once the children heard it, they would hustle to the sound so we could give them directions.

We were nothing like Captain von Trapp from *The Sound of Music* or Mr. Gilbreth from *Cheaper by the Dozen* with military-like order, but in many ways, ours was an orderly home. Our children listened to instruction and were quick to help, but we also enjoyed freedom and creativity inside of those structures. Our early homeschool days were smooth; everyone quickly did their chores in the morning so we could head out to our little schoolroom with a bowl of fresh sliced apples to munch on during our lessons. Afternoons were spent playing by the shallow creek with the tall pines standing watch overhead, or caring for our animals and the garden. It was a beautiful life.

It's hard to pinpoint when order first began to erode in our home. When we moved back to the United States after four years as missionaries, we were weary and disillusioned, and my husband was especially discouraged. He had loved his life of service, loved working with his kids each day on projects for the orphanage, and struggled to find equilibrium in the new job that took him away from his family for several weeks at a time. My children were trying to find their place in the community after being gone for four years, and I was having my own growing pains settling into life with a new baby and managing a home while my husband worked out of town. All of us were dealing with some degree of sadness, which made it difficult to establish order, but what really catapulted our family into a whole new level of pain was the eating disorder that was torturing our daughter. It felt as though we were on a high-speed train to hell and couldn't get off. Every decision we made created even more pain, and we couldn't figure out how to get out of the hole. Each crisis precipitated more problems, and our family suffered even more as my husband and I failed to lead. We felt inadequate and disqualified, which opened us up to bad advice that created even more problems.

In an effort to correct my mistakes that I thought had led us to this point, I started reading books that suggested giving more choices to young children, books indicating that young children could decide for themselves. Not only was I confused about how to parent in light of my daughter's struggle, but I was also distracted from parenting. Those of you who are parenting a wide range of ages will understand this struggle. It grew harder and harder to filter out the adult world for our younger children when some of our older children were becoming adults. This meant that instead of whistling roll call and teaching the children to obey instructions as a group, I was trying to parent several different stages at once: toddlers, preteens, and young adults. What this looked like was my saying yes to nearly everything the little ones asked for and failing to consistently follow through on habit training because of a lack of confidence and attention. I was distracted by my sense of failure, my confusion, and a sense of inadequacy.

The Word of God Is a Better Guide

Rather than turning to modern parenting guides, I should have turned to the Word of God in that season. Colossians 3:18–21 lays out a simple structure for family life that modern teachers have largely ignored:

> Wives, submit to your husbands, as is fitting in the Lord. Husbands, love your wives and do not be harsh with them. Children, obey your parents in everything, for this pleases the Lord. Fathers, do not provoke your children, lest they become discouraged.

There is a holistic picture here of order with gentleness and love, and sticking to that structure in faith would have saved us a lot of heartache.

But sometimes we need concrete examples of obedience and order, and Elisabeth Elliot and Susan Schaeffer Macaulay are two authors who showed me through their words. The idea that there are structures of authority is often a foreign concept to modern people and rarely talked about, even in Christian circles. Susan Schaeffer Macaulay understood this struggle. As the daughter of Francis and Edith Schaeffer, she grew up listening to students question authority structures as well as norms of civility, and saw them embrace rebellion. She was no stranger to the modern struggle we face; society has deemed us all free to do what we want, to pursue our own best selves. No longer is there social pressure for children to obey parents or for wives to honor their husbands. And the reality is that autonomy does not nurture happy homes or restored communities. Autonomy, or every man for himself, is partly to blame for the breakdown in culture we are currently witnessing. An article from I.Family describes autonomy in this way, "In its simplest sense, autonomy is about a person's ability to act on his or her own values and interests. Taken from ancient Greek, the word means 'self-legislation' or 'self-governance.' Modern political thought and bioethics often stress that individual autonomy should be promoted and respected."[1]

Self-legislation is something we all should aim for, but when culture has deemed everyone acting in their own best interest as the highest goal, we are headed for trouble. Children are dependent and need people willing to set aside their own best interests to care for them. Susan Schaeffer Macaulay had heard these same arguments and recognized the danger of living with oneself as the highest arbiter of law. In her book *For the Family's Sake: The Value of Home in Everyone's Life*, she begins with a chapter on order. She believed that cultures could be redeemed by returning to basic Christian principles and rejecting the nihilism that was destroying civilization. She believed that being legislated by God and his Word instead of by our own desires and interests is the true path to joy. This aligns with what Saint Benedict wrote, based on Psalm 119:32, in the prologue to his rule: "We shall run on the path of God's commandments, our hearts overflowing with the inexpressible delight of love."[2]

I love this picture of willingly putting ourselves under the authority of God and staying on his path not out of fear but out of love. If we are in Christ, we no longer have to fear being rejected by God when we make a mistake, but we must realize that submission to God's ways is not only commanded, but it also brings life and joy and peace. We may not be destined for hell if we break the Sabbath or tell a lie, because we have the chance to confess our sins and receive forgiveness, but the law of sowing and reaping is still in effect. If we gossip, people will gossip about us. If we hate our parents, our children will hate us. If we are disrespectful to our husband, our children will be disrespectful to us. As modern Christians, many of us have become apathetic about obedience when, in fact, our confidence in the work of Jesus should lead us to pursue holiness. Many Christians focus on their own comfort and pleasure ahead of higher goals such as transforming homes and culture. Susan Schaeffer Macaulay witnessed this in her time as well, writing, "Believers who know they are safe and forgiven can become casual about goodness and obedience. It becomes easy then to break rules without trying too hard to obey. When we start doing wrong, the practice escalates, becoming a habit. Wrongdoing hardens a person."[3]

And culture has intentionally made us leery of concepts like order and obedience. Karl Marx and Friedrich Engels, the originators of Marxist philosophy, believed that traditional concepts of family life were an impediment to the abolition of private property. They fought for communal raising of children as a means to that end. In an article about their beliefs from *The History of European Ideas*, Richard Weikart writes,

> Furthermore, Marx and Engels provided some hints in *The Communist Manifesto* concerning the social relations that would

supersede the family. First they discussed the status of children, whose exploitation they wanted to end. They proposed the replacement of home education by social education (*Erziehung*), which included, but encompassed far more than, sending children to public schools. The German term *Erziehung* entails not only formal education, but any training of children, including that normally given by parents. Marx and Engels reinforced their point further by assaulting the "bourgeois claptrap about the family and education, about the hallowed co-relation of parent and child." Furthermore, Engels in his draft for *The Communist Manifesto* articulated more clearly his vision for children in communist society: "The raising (*Erziehung*) of children together in national institutions and at national expense, from that moment on, in which they can dispense with the first motherly care."[4]

It's easy to see this contempt for family sovereignty and traditional family structures being promoted in culture today. For years, television and movies have ridiculed fathers and promoted the idea that children know best. The press rarely points to the lack of a traditional family as being a culprit in societal ills; if a fatherless child becomes a school shooter, his or her parental status is seldom mentioned. On the other hand, Christian families or pastors with moral failings are more likely to become front-page headlines or the subject of podcast series. None of this is accidental, but it's been so slow and subtle that it can be hard to detect. I myself have been guilty of ridiculing Christians who don't conform to worldly measures of cool, and I've definitely been disrespectful to my husband, disregarding a biblical admonishment to give honor. But this promotion of mutual ridicule and disrespect instead of mutual love is intentional too. In his book *Rules for Radicals*, which he dedicated to the first radical, Lucifer, Saul Alinsky writes, "*Ridicule is man's most potent weapon*. It is almost impossible to counterattack ridicule. Also it infuriates the opposition, who then react to your advantage."[5]

There Is a Better Way

It's clear in the Bible, the Orthodox Jews have been prioritizing it for millennia and preserving their culture, and it was one of the three core values of the Benedictines: obedience. Order is one of the ways we save civilization, and it's essential for Christians. Susan Schaeffer Macaulay explains it this way: "The God of creation tells the creature what the rules of operation are. Just as airplanes cannot fly unless they follow the laws of aerodynamics, so we are eventually 'grounded' when we ignore the basic rules of life to do whatever seems interesting."[6]

So one step toward a sacred home, a home that is centered on restoration of hope and intimacy with God, is restoring our reverence for the Word of God. Returning to God's structures may mean not listening to all the stories of Christians who have failed, and refusing to let ourselves be disillusioned from faith because a pastor abused his position of leadership or because a church family failed to support us through a hardship. It's learning to forgive those who have trespassed against us, instead of holding them in judgment and as a result turning away from God. We do live in a fallen world, and it's easy to find examples of people who thought they were obeying God's Word but ended up creating havoc.

In one town, a woman used her position of authority at a Christian school to sexually abuse teenage girls. A chaplain abandoned his wife and six children, claiming that God told him to do so. I understand the destruction that comes when people in authority abuse the trust we have put in them. It happened in my own family when a pastor cursed and castigated my father for wanting to move away from his hometown. I understand some of this pain. The world would want us to channel that pain into hatred, ridicule, and victimhood. The enemy of our souls would tempt us to turn away from God and live for ourselves. But God has a better way, and we can see it in the lives of his people who turn away from bitterness and allow the Holy Spirit to lead them in paths of righteousness.

Elisabeth Elliot was no stranger to tragic pain and loss. She waited five years from the day she met her husband, Jim Elliot, until they could be married because he was busy establishing his life as a missionary and trying to discern if marriage was right for him. She simply continued her education and waited for him to be ready. They were finally married in 1953, and settled into their jungle home in Ecuador where they did missionary work. Their first child arrived a couple years later, in February of 1955, and they spent a happy summer enjoying family life at the mission station. By the fall of that year, Jim Elliot had started reaching out to the Huaorani people—also called the Auca, an indigenous Ecuadorian group considered violent and dangerous to outsiders. He and four other missionaries would fly over their village and drop small gifts while relaying messages of love. They had to use patience and caution because the Huaorani were known to kill anyone who attempted contact with them. Finally, one day in January of 1956, they landed their plane on a nearby beach and spent some hours attempting to converse with three people from the tribe. It seemed that their dream of reaching them for Jesus was finally coming true, as the natives received the missionaries with curiosity and kindness. The three Huaorani headed on the path back to their camp while Jim and the four other missionaries stayed by the plane, hoping for more opportunities to connect. Tragically, the next group of natives who visited them on the beach were warriors. They speared all five of the missionaries to death and ransacked their plane.

Elisabeth faced a choice in that tragic, heart-wrenching season. She could have easily become bitter toward God, resentful toward mission work, and hardhearted about marriage. She had waited five years from the time she met Jim to marry him, and then, only three years into their marriage, he was dead, impaled with a spear. Perhaps she experienced moments like Jesus' temptation in the desert or when Satan tempted Adam and Eve in the Garden— that moment of palpable weakness when the enemy of our soul whispers, "Did God really say . . . ?" or "Was serving God really worth it?" or "Does God really love you?"

Elisabeth chose to believe that God loved her and had good plans for her. She had chosen God and she wasn't going to try to take back her surrender after the loss of her husband. She wrote, "Any 'soldier,' any candidate for Christian discipline, ought daily to report to his commanding officer for duty. At your service, Lord. What the soldier does for the officer is not in the category of a favor. The officer may ask anything. He disposes of the soldier as he chooses."[7]

She wasn't offended at God for taking her husband because she had already willingly given him up. She recognized God as Lord and had taken to heart the words of her husband, Jim: "He is no fool who gives what he cannot keep to gain that which he cannot lose."[8]

So rather than rejecting God and biblical Christian values because of the loss of her husband, Elisabeth doubled down on devotion. In her lifetime she wrote more than thirty-five books, several of them with themes of order and discipline. She even returned to the Huaorani people who murdered her husband to share the gospel with them, with her young daughter in tow. Her love of and devotion to God and her willingness to obey him at any cost were the motivating forces in her life, and her writing has encouraged countless Christians with the same message. In describing the importance of obedience to God's authority, she writes,

> The goal of the cook—a perfect dessert—will not be attained without her first giving up her "right" to do it her way, then studying the book and doing exactly what it says. . . .
>
> Why then instead of taking Christ at His word, do we prefer to argue . . . to claim our "rights," to muddle through on our own? In this way paradise was lost.[9]

And while obedience is clearly extolled in Scripture (it is mentioned ninety-five times hand in hand with the blessings of obedience), it is hard to live out. Jesus said,

If anyone would come after me, let him deny himself and take up
his cross and follow me. For whoever would save his life will lose
it, but whoever loses his life for my sake will find it. For what will
it profit a man if he gains the whole world and forfeits his soul?
Or what shall a man give in return for his soul?

Matthew 16:24–26

The call to obedience to God's Word is clear both in the stories and in the verses. Daniel was honored and rescued because
he obeyed God rather than the king, but he had to endure a long
night in a lion's den; Shadrach, Meshach, and Abednego were
saved from a fiery furnace because they refused to bow down to an
idol, choosing to suffer for God rather than be honored by men.
Jesus, who lived a perfect life as God's son, obeyed his Father in
tears and anguish on the night of his arrest, saying, "Not my will,
but yours, be done" (Luke 22:42).

While obedience may seem like the opposite of world-saving,
and often feels more mortifying than life-giving, God promises he
will bless us when we obey. As the Benedictines also recognized
their need and dependence on God, I think monastery life can give
us a picture of how we can apply obedience to our own modern
homes. According to Saint Benedict, obedience is the first step of
humility and "comes naturally to those who cherish Christ above
all. Because of the holy service they have professed, or because of
the dread of hell and for the glory of everlasting life, they carry
out the superior's order as promptly as if the command came
from God himself."[10]

Establishing Order After Disappointment

Many of today's second-generation homeschoolers were raised
in families that tried to practice a monastery-like existence, with
clear authority structures and a separateness from the world, but
bitterness grew as they witnessed their parents' failures. As well,

many of the fathers in these groups were accountable to no one, which left the wives and children in peril, and maybe even angry with God for not delivering them from an angry or selfish father. In my own family, I had read books about submissive womanhood and respecting your husband as the head of the home; I tried to obey God's Word, but ultimately my fear was a louder voice, and my laid-back husband let me take over. I ended up carrying a much bigger burden than I asked for. The more I made decisions for the family, the more decisions my husband didn't have to make, and the more aware I became of how heavy a burden that was. It left me exhausted, suffering from adrenal fatigue, and trying to make too many parental decisions on my own. It became a snowball, growing enormous by picking up the mess in its path and it threatened to destroy our family. I've written extensively about this season in *Mothering by the Book*, but it's worth repeating that once we had worked through forgiveness and reconciliation, and rejected identifying as victims, regaining a healthy sense of structure was one of the keys to getting back on our feet as a family.

Reading the words of Elisabeth Elliot encouraged my heart in the struggle, because order does not come easily for me. In fact, when I told my husband I was writing a chapter about obedience, he laughed. One of his key phrases to describe me is that I'm a force to be reckoned with. But Elisabeth, who was also a strong and determined woman, had a message of order and obedience that stayed consistent despite the loss of two husbands (her second husband died of cancer). She didn't grow bitter and reject Scripture and make up her own set of values; she stayed steadfast to obey God, despite the disappointments of her life. She truly understood the exhortation to "Set your affection on things above, not on things on the earth. For ye are dead, and your life is hid with Christ in God. When Christ, who is our life, shall appear, then shall ye also appear with him in glory" (Colossians 3:2–4 kjv). Although she had suffered tragic loss, she continued to turn her heart toward God.

But what does order look like for modern families today? How do we apply biblical advice from thousands of years ago, or even monastic advice from 1,500 years ago, to our lives? Maybe it starts with just a few small adjustments in our thinking. Most of you reading this book are mothers who are caring for children in your home. You naturally want them to be whole people who can have a happy life. But this does not mean that easy is best! Even from a scientific perspective, grit and self-control are important keys to happiness, along with connection to other humans. So you have the responsibility to teach your children self-control and grit too. You have the calling to teach your children to be able to follow directions from a teacher or boss, to be able to survive a difficult situation, to be able to thrive under adverse circumstances. You have a responsibility to teach them to care about others and to not think only about their own pleasure.

We've all seen the destruction to culture when people are too fragile, easily offended, and self-absorbed. Culture falls apart quickly when people are unable to follow directions or care about others, so there is an imperative to teach biblical character qualities to your children. However, discipline and order have been so mocked that it can feel awkward even to expect them of our own children. Dennis Okholm, the author of *Monk Habits for Everyday People*, writes that obedience is "almost a dirty word outside of military schools. But it really needs to be part of the Christian's vocabulary."[11]

We know that more is caught than taught, as the saying goes, so consider how you live out self-control, perseverance, and other necessary characteristics in your own life. Are you able to stay in a relationship with people who are difficult? I'm not talking about staying in an abusive relationship, but do you have the grit to work through issues in relationships or do you always walk away? Can you follow directions from others and be a team player? Are you able to exercise humility or are you constantly feeling victimized by those around you? Are you kind and respectful to your husband? Do you blame others for your problems or are you self-aware and working on your issues? It's important to teach our children to follow basic instructions for orderly living if we are going to be a part of restoring culture. The instructions to the abbot of a monastery from Saint Benedict himself give insight into how to be a great leader of our own little flock:

> The abbot . . . must know what a difficult and demanding burden he has undertaken; directing souls and serving a variety of temperaments, coaxing, reproving, and encouraging them as appropriate. He must so accommodate and adapt himself to each one's character and intelligence. . . . [H]e has undertaken the care of souls for whom he must give account.[12]

The passage sounds like the description of a mother in the home. We are called to a difficult and demanding burden, and it takes a high level of self-forgetfulness to love well. In my case, loving and leading my children has been much easier than following my husband and letting him lead. However, if I'm trying to teach my children to obey both their parents and God, then I must work toward honoring my husband and modeling for my children what I expect from them. If I want my children to obey God's Word, then I need to meditate on it daily and live it.

I have the freedom to disregard the law of sowing and reaping, to be manipulative and bossy with my husband while trying to teach my children to love and honor me, to be self-centered and grasping while trying to teach my children to be loving and kind. However, even if I ignore the law of sowing and reaping, it is still there, doing its quiet duty of producing the fruit that we ourselves have sown. Living with order doesn't mean we put ourselves under the authority of cult leaders or obey ungodly laws. It doesn't mean we don't have a say in our home and family life, waiting passively for our husband to make all the decisions and refusing to steward our gifts and calling. Scripture clearly declares that "we must obey God rather than men" (Acts 5:29), that we have been given authority as women to manage our sphere of influence (1 Timothy 5:14), and that we are created in the image of God (Genesis 1:27), with all the creativity and authority that entails. So this isn't a call to become a doormat, just letting life happen to us. Instead, check your heart. Can you show honor while still having healthy boundaries? Can you obey Scripture without being manipulated by an overbearing church leader? Can you learn to be in a close and listening relationship with God so you can navigate living according to the Word of God thousands of years after it was written? Acting in opposition to God's Word won't result in restoration; we need Holy Spirit discernment to know how to apply it today.

> Being under the authority of God's Word empowers us to live with authority over tyrants, bad habits, and beloved children.

If we feel the world outside is chaotic, let's sow peace in our home. If we feel the world outside is cruel, our homes should be islands of kindness; if we feel that people are selfish and grasping, we should model love and generosity. We reap what we sow, and God promises to reward us for our obedience to his Word. Our salvation is secure in Jesus, but our families become a force for restoration in the world when we love and honor God's Word. Being under the authority of God's Word empowers us to live with authority over tyrants, bad habits, and beloved children. Anarchy creates chaos and destruction, but order brings peace. As we surrender to God and obey his Word, we see him more clearly, and it's in his presence that true freedom is found.

STUDY GUIDE

How have you experienced the principle of order?

Is it hard for you to live with rules?

Is order a value you want to cultivate in your home?

Habits of Order: Add to the list below and then use the list to make your own family rule.

Be respectful to others.
Follow reasonable directions.
Be discerning.
Pray for people in positions of authority.
Be orderly with your belongings.
Develop a daily rhythm.
Track your habits.

What habits will you adopt in your family? For example, your statements about order might be:

In the _____ family, we listen attentively when another is speaking.
In the _____ family, we obey God's Word.

Or write your own here:

_____

_____

When you have decided on your statement about habits of order, you can plug it into the Your Rule of Life template in the appendix.

A VERSE TO MEMORIZE

You shall walk in all the way that the Lord your God has commanded you, that you may live, and that it may go well with you, and that you may live long in the land that you shall possess.

Deuteronomy 5:33

A PRAYER

Dear God, thank you for loving me and for providing redemption through Jesus. I confess that I have disobeyed your Word in big and small ways, and I want to turn away from trusting in worldly philosophies and turn toward you. Please help me to be discerning and to know what your will is. Please give me the strength to obey you.

FURTHER READING

Joyful Surrender: 7 Disciplines for the Believer's Life by Elisabeth Elliot
The Shaping of a Christian Family: How My Parents Nurtured My Faith by Elisabeth Elliot
Through Gates of Splendor by Elisabeth Elliot

A RECIPE

Taco Soup

1 pound ground beef
1 medium diced onion
4 cloves minced garlic
1 15½-ounce can pinto beans
1 15½-ounce can white beans
1 15¼-ounce can whole kernel
  corn, drained
2 14½-ounce cans diced
  tomatoes
1 4½-ounce can diced green
  chiles
2 cups water
1 teaspoon beef bouillon

1 teaspoon salt
½ teaspoon chili powder
½ teaspoon dried oregano
½ teaspoon paprika
1½ teaspoons ground cumin

Corn chips
Sour cream
Grated cheese
Chopped green onions
Chopped cilantro
Pickled jalapeños

PREP: 20 minutes COOK: 60 minutes TOTAL: 80 minutes

1. Brown the ground beef, onion, and garlic in a large skillet.

2. Drain the excess fat, then transfer the meat mixture to a large slow cooker.

3. Add the beans, corn, tomatoes, green chiles, water, and seasonings.

4. Cook in a slow cooker on low for 6 to 8 hours.

5. Serve with corn chips, sour cream, cheese, chopped green onions, chopped cilantro, and pickled jalapeños.

Serves 6

6

HABITS OF SIMPLICITY

Sabina Wurmbrand

> While others quarreled and fought, we lay on our mattresses and
> used the Bible for prayer and meditation, and repeated its verses
> to ourselves through the long nights.
>
> Sabina Wurmbrand, *The Pastor's Wife*

The week after the holidays is one of my favorite weeks of the
year. I love taking the time to rest, organize, and begin to plan
the new year. This year was different, however. My husband and
I and our two youngest children were moving away for a couple
months to be near one of our adult children, and the detached
apartment on our property where my oldest daughter lives was
going to be an Airbnb while she lived in the main house. All this
shuffling around meant moving our youngest son out of his room
to make room for our daughter. While it was a lot of work to put
new flooring into the detached apartment, install curtains and a

new vanity, and filter through our books to make sure we sanitized them for the general public (*The Kingdom of Cults* was probably not a good Airbnb title), the biggest job was cleaning out my son's room. There were Legos under the bed and in the closet, books stuffed in drawers, three dressers full of odds and ends including dead batteries, matchbox cars, half-filled journals, miniature volcano models, geodes, and Playmobil weapons, not to mention empty Lego boxes and instruction manuals stacked in the closet. It took a full day to sort, pack, discard, and fit the remaining items back into his half of the closet.

A full day. A day of my life that I spent sneezing my way through the mountain of dust, a day that I spent frustrated with my son for not maintaining his belongings better, a day that ended with my yelling at him and threatening to give away all his stuff (not an idle threat, since by the end of the day, I had sold an entire bin of Legos on Facebook Marketplace for a mere ten dollars just to get them out of my sight). Through it all, my son was unperturbed, barely stirring himself to look at the belongings I had pulled from every corner before piling it all in the middle of his room. Birthday presents, new-school-year gifts, and even things purchased with money he had earned had lost their charm. At the end of the day, he was relieved to be taking just one suitcase and box to the house we would be staying in, happy to be freed from caring for all these meaningless bits of plastic.

And yet, as we arrived at the Airbnb and I settled my own three bins of books, one suitcase of clothes, and Nespresso machine into the small home, I felt a little bereft. My days at home were so full with homeschooling, working on life-giving homeschool resources for The Peaceful Press, connecting with adult children, and managing my home and garden that I was often stretched thin, ending up weary after keeping the plates spinning all day. The contrast of being in a home that I did not own, surrounded by art I did not choose, and without even a single plant to care for made me uncomfortable. I felt lonely, whether for my beautiful light-filled home or for my adult daughters who had stayed behind I'm not sure, but there was an unsettled feeling that I couldn't quite shake. There was a void.

The work of home I was used to was limitless and interconnected. For example, once I finished painting the house, I needed to put all the books back. Once the books were all put back, I could tackle the laundry room. Once the laundry room was organized, I needed to organize my clothes and reorder the jeans and shirts and sweaters back into their places. On and on it went, one job leading to another with my time at home pressed with the need to organize our things.

Now I found myself in an Airbnb for a few months with nothing to organize, no fridge full of sourdough and kombucha to care for, and no garden to weed. In short, I had nothing to do besides homeschool my children, work on my computer, and pray. My daily chores were simple: plan and shop for dinner and teach the two children with me how to cook and clean up after themselves. Do the laundry. Homeschool. I had been so busy for so long that it felt awkward to suddenly have more time on my hands and less to manage. In addition, my schedule was suddenly very empty. In my hometown I am fortunate to have many friends, so I constantly feel that I could be doing more to stay connected with each of them. And then there is the weekly schedule of homeschool activities that include co-op, music lessons, and nature group. Now I had nothing on the schedule—I was in a new town, and my weeks were wide open with space for taking long walks or trying new recipes. But having nothing to take care of and nowhere to go was uncomfortable. I was sorely tempted to just abandon this little adventure and head back home.

Restoration Requires Simplicity

But restoration of the beautiful and the sacred in culture requires a certain level of simplicity. When we continue in a mindless round of buying stuff and organizing it, of filling our schedule so that every day passes in a whirl of activity, we end up leaving no space for intentionality. We can't live counterculturally when we don't even have mental space to evaluate what that means for us, or how the values of the day are affecting us. Restoration requires reflection and time to evaluate what is working well and what is working to destroy us. If we don't step back and look at our lives, we won't know what needs to change.

> We can't live counterculturally when we don't even have mental space to evaluate what that means for us, or how the values of the day are affecting us.

But we love our stuff. I felt physically uncomfortable in the Airbnb without my familiar surroundings, without my plants and pets and favorite mugs and cozy bed. Even though my husband and two of my children were with me, I still felt homesick. Some of this is reasonable since my own home is surrounded by beautiful nature, and the meaningful work of refreshing sourdough and weeding the garden is good for my soul. But Saint Benedict strongly warned against private ownership, writing,

> Above all others, let this vice be extirpated in the monastery. No one, without leave of the abbot, shall presume to give, or receive, or keep as his own, anything whatever: neither book, nor tablets, nor pen: nothing at all. For monks are men who can claim no dominion even over their own bodies or wills.[1]

As an American, the idea of owning nothing is abhorrent to me, and I scoffed when the World Economic Forum promoted the idea that by 2030 people will own nothing and be happy. I've read about the long history of suffering under totalitarian governments: Central planning and central ownership usually mean suffering for many and luxury for few. However, I think there are two different thought processes that are important to understand so we can come to our own version of simplicity. In the case of the Benedictines, private ownership implied that the monks were their own, with their own things to dispose of at will. Yet they had consecrated themselves to God and taken vows that declared they were no longer their own, but God's. So the conscious action of not owning anything was their way of acknowledging utter dependence on God. It was a daily surrender that they freely offered, not compulsory poverty. In the words of the Heidelberg Catechism, "I, with body and soul, both in life and in death, am not my own, but belong to my faithful Savior Jesus Christ."[2]

Sabina Wurmbrand was a Christian woman from Romania who had lost everything because of Soviet communism. You could say that she endured forced simplicity, rather than the chosen simplicity of the Benedictine monks. A government, removed from the laws laid out in the Bible, will never make fully just decisions about who deserves a food ration card and who doesn't. The communist fervor to destroy religion and remove all traces of God meant they were especially cruel to people of faith. Communist leaders were so suspicious that no one was safe. A valued party member could be living in the comparative luxury that accompanied that status, but the next day could be thrown in jail because a jealous co-worker denounced him. For the majority of families living in the Soviet Bloc, daily life was a struggle. The government didn't provide enough food, and if you were a political prisoner or married to one, you weren't allowed a food ration card or a job. The simple life these people experienced was not our romantic ideal.

Sabina was the wife of a pastor, a Jew by ethnicity who had survived the Nazi occupation of Romania, only to be arrested and imprisoned in the early 1950s under the communists. She and her husband, Richard, had come to Christ in 1936, and they experienced the joy that comes from his presence. Sabina had been no stranger to the good life, enjoying parties and luxuries in prewar

Romania, but she knew that Jesus was better. They spent the years of World War II sharing the gospel in Romania, and when the war ended, they continued their work of distributing Christian literature. When an opportunity came for Sabina and her husband to flee Romania and the communists, knowing that to remain almost certainly meant imprisonment or death, they chose to stay. They didn't want to miss a chance to share the love of God with their people. It was worth giving up comfort and material possessions to gain Jesus, and she and her husband, Richard, truly understood that "a day in your courts is better than a thousand elsewhere" (Psalm 84:10).

But they wrestled over the decision to stay, knowing what it would mean for their son. In her book *The Pastor's Wife*, she writes that while it was not yet too late to leave the country,

> I knew that Richard didn't really want to go but he said:
> "Under Antonescu's rule we were never imprisoned for more than two to three weeks at a time. With the Communists, it can last for years. And they may take you too. And Mihai—who will look after him, and the other children?"[3]

Sabina knew the horrors that could await them if they stayed in Romania. A woman who had been sent to a Siberian labor camp for twelve years had recently visited the Wurmbrands. She described being forced to stand barefoot on ice for hours after being caught telling others about Jesus, and enduring starvation and tortures that continued during her years as a captive. This visitor warned Sabina of the future they could expect if they were caught sharing Christ as pastors in a communist country, but Sabina's message to her husband was full of faith. She said,

> I . . . opened the Scripture where Jesus says: "Whosoever will save his life shall lose it and whosoever will lose his life for my sake will find it."

I asked Richard, "If you leave now, will you ever be able again to preach about this text?"[4]

While the Wurmbrands weren't Benedictine monks, they lived the same lifestyle of absolute surrender of their possessions and their lives to God. When the opportunity came to leave Romania to save themselves and their son, they chose to stay for the sake of the gospel and for the sake of their love for God. But they suffered for their choice. Richard was imprisoned for fourteen years and Sabina for three; she spent her time as a captive encouraging other prisoners in the Lord, reciting Scripture, leading prayers, and telling of the love of Jesus. She shares the story of one fellow prisoner:

> The daughter of a high Communist official, herself a Christian, learnt one evening that she must face the firing squad at midnight.
> . . .
> As the girl was taken out, she raised her voice in the Creed. . . . The words were those we say in church. But it was a different Creed, because she meant every word. She went to death for the one God, and was received into life everlasting.[5]

A Willing Sacrifice

They were willing to give up their lives for the gospel, but the suffering they endured was great. Forced to work long hours in the field, planting crops by hand, or moving rocks to build a canal with no water or food for the entire day, were just some of many hardships. Not being able to care for their families was a terrible loss. The women in prison fretted about the children who were left behind, worrying about who was caring for them and how they were surviving. And while under communism they had already lived with few material possessions, they experienced new levels of deprivation, and even the joy of working for their families was taken from them. In the first few weeks of prison, while the women were waiting for their labor assignments, they anguished about the life they had taken for granted. As Wurmbrand observed, "Women talked with longing about cooking and cleaning. How they would like to bake a cake for their children. . . . A mother understands when the children leave home what a joy working for them was, what wretchedness it is to have nothing to do."[6]

We aren't currently being asked to suffer in this way, and I tell these stories not to shame us for the bounty we live with, but to help us gain perspective. Simplicity is a virtue that can be hard to cultivate in our world of plenty. My home is full of items for me to organize; there are closets to clean out and kitchen cupboards to arrange. I received new baking sheets as a gift, and I need to find a place to put them and drop my old ones off at Goodwill. I wanted new workout clothes but needed to sort through what I already had and make space for them. Small purchases create ripple effects of new work we must manage, and it squeezes out time for connection with our children, making a meal for a new mom, or having a fun conversation with our husband. Our overly full lives prevent restoration when we become stuff managers. We aren't "the restorer of streets to dwell in" we are called to be in Isaiah 58:12; instead, we are full-time closet organizers.

But there are simple things we can do to work toward simplicity and to reorder our priorities so restoration in our families and communities can take its proper place. Even my simple transition to an Airbnb where I had only a few things to manage helped me see the fruit of a simpler life. I suddenly had more time to teach good habits to my children, or just sit and chat with them, and more time to hug my husband and be friendly. I wasn't drowning with piles of things to sort, and I could make the people in my life the principal focus of my attention. A mother in a chair with nothing in her hands is such a rare vision, it's a picture of a human who is present and attentive to the world around her, and it is a gift to our families to take at least some time each day to be that present. Simplicity is the path to that place.

Simplicity as a Path to Presence

What are the steps to simplify so we can have that kind of presence? So we make time for people?

1. **Limit screen time**—Whether it is a phone in your hand, a television, or a computer, screens steal our attention and make it hard for us to connect. I've gone to my bedroom to clean and organize it, only to find myself picking up my phone to start listening to a podcast and then getting sucked into the loop of checking email, social media, and even my health app. Our phones are a tremendous time suck, and our brains are so used to the constant input that it's a struggle to put the phone down. But work on incorporating screen-free days, screen-free evenings, and regular screen sabbaticals. Set screen time limits, get an accountability partner, or do whatever is necessary to make your phone a tool, not a master.

2. **Limit shopping**—While online shopping can be a way we boost our serotonin and produce some joy, that feeling doesn't last and it costs us hours of time that could be spent creating or connecting. When we purchase something, we invest precious time browsing, researching, and comparing prices. Then there is time spent disposing of the packaging, adding to burgeoning landfills. Once we have it in our homes, we must maintain it: wash, sort, fold, organize in an endless cycle. Instead, learn to make lists of things we think we need and then sit on that list for a bit to see if we can do without it. It also takes money, which represents more hours of our time working instead of being present with our family. Schedule your shopping time instead of just purchasing whenever you get a whim, and when you bring something new into your home, let something else go. We can trust that God will provide.

While there is wisdom in preparation, we don't put our
faith in things.

3. **Use what you have**—When a sale email comes through
   our inbox or we are browsing Sephora, it's easy to get
   excited about something new even though we have plenty
   at home. I've bought new lotion even though I had five
   half-filled bottles at home. I've bought new books even
   though I was in the middle of several. I've bought new
   candles even though I already had a few in the cupboard
   waiting to be used. All this does is teach us to gratify our
   wants immediately and create more stuff for us to manage. Instead of buying new things when you want them,
   try waiting until you need them, especially in regard to
   nonessentials or luxury items. (Keeping an extra package
   of bath tissue or rice on hand is just wise preparation—
   having twenty different lipsticks, not so much).

4. **Curate the schedule**—Simplicity in our lives can create
   more time for connection and therefore restoration, but
   when we are overscheduled, rushing in and out of the
   door, chaos ensues. Busyness creates stress and steals the
   time we need to be stewards of our home and loving shep-
   herds of our children. It also often masks inner turmoil.
   We avoid being alone with our thoughts or our children
   because of unrest that we haven't worked through. If you
   are running away from your own thoughts, *Mothering by
   the Book* can help you evaluate them and gain freedom
   from your fears, which will empower you to simplify the
   schedule. Restoration takes time, and if we don't keep a
   healthy rhythm of work, rest, and prayer, then the time to
   connect with God, ourselves, and others simply won't be
   available.

5. **Own less**—The Benedictines owned nothing, and Sabina
   Wurmbrand lost everything when she went to prison for

her faith. We don't have to be extreme, but fewer possessions do equal fewer decisions, making more time for love.
When our closets are full, it takes longer to decide what to
wear. When our pantries are full, it takes longer to decide
what to cook. When our bookshelves are full, we have
more to sort through. Simply owning fewer things can
create more time for meaningful relationships, and it's in
healthy connections that restoration happens.

6. **Don't accumulate debt**—From the beginning of our marriage, my husband and I made a commitment to live debt-
free. We drove old cars (yes, they broke down sometimes),
wore whatever clothes we had while friends were constantly showing up in new outfits, and didn't replace our
electronics just because new versions had come out. Living
below our means became a lifestyle choice for us, which
meant that when the chance came to fulfill our dream
of missions, we had the resources to do so. It also meant
that we were able to fulfill our dream of having a country
property with acres of woods for our children to explore.
We didn't spend all we made on our daily life, and thus
that margin between our income and our expenses created
space for more peace. It also contributed to restoration.
Because we spent less than we earned, we could take a
family vacation to connect with our children, or pay for a
marriage conference so we could connect better as a couple. Restoration is an investment, and if we are tapped out
storing up treasure on earth, we won't have the time or
money to sow into eternal relationships and eternal values.

So much of the pursuit of restoration requires anchoring our
identity in Christ. Sabina Wurmbrand was able to resist the destructive values of her communist oppressors because she knew
the truth and wasn't swayed by propaganda. When her son came
home from school repeating the horror stories the communists

had told him about the church and clergy, she could respond with Scripture instead of becoming embittered toward her faith. When the choice was set before them to turn their back on God so they could live in comfort, they chose to suffer for Christ rather than deny their faith. When the authorities tried to tempt Sabina to divorce her imprisoned husband so her child would have better opportunities for school and work, she resisted their offers. She had tasted and seen that the Lord is good, that in his presence are pleasures forevermore, and she knew that the enjoyment of silk stockings and fine wine was temporary. The communists eventually fell, destroyed by their godless system, but the families who continue to honor God will be honored, either (or both) in this life or the next.

Maybe the things that try to steal your affections are not the same as those Sabina Wurmbrand faced, but there are always distractions we must fight against in our pursuit of restoration in culture. We've created our own escape valves for when our relationships are hard, but these escape valves steal our peace. When we feel worried about a relationship, we might turn to online shopping instead of prayer. When we are unhappy with ourselves, we try to stuff down the feelings by staying extra busy. Our children's behavior seems unmanageable, so we hide in the laundry room scrolling social media. This cycle of pain avoidance actually makes our life more painful. We can simplify by bringing God into our pain. As we learn to invite God into our anguish and disappointment, to bring our conflicts and our struggles to him for his perspective on the situation, we can begin to live with a simple trusting heart.

So much of the chaos in our world—the homelessness and addiction, the broken relationships and conflict—is the result of unhealed pain, of people stuck in fear and shame, and then masking it through activities that only perpetuate that pain. But when we simplify and stop using busyness and material things to mask our unrest and instead enter into a lifestyle of connection to God, we can see our families transformed, and cultural restoration is simply the fruit of healthy families.

WHEN YOU FEEL . . .	INSTEAD OF . . .	TRY THIS . . .
Unrest	instead of immediately numbing out with your addiction of choice	try just sitting with God and speaking Scripture over yourself.
Afraid because a child is misbehaving again, and you start imagining the trouble they will have in the future	instead of masking it through online shopping	try writing about how you feel in your journal and saying a prayer.
Lonely and left out	instead of scrolling through social media	try taking a walk in nature, calling your mom, or taking a meal to a friend.

Simplifying requires facing our pain. The beauty of learning to sit through pain is that we get more of God as a result. In his book *Addiction and Grace*, author Gerald May writes,

The specific struggles we undergo with our addictions are reflections of a blessed pain. To be deprived of a simple object of attachment is to taste the deep, holy deprivation of our souls. To struggle to transcend any idol is to touch the sacred hunger God has given us. In such a light, what we have called asceticism is no longer a way of dealing with attachment, but an act of love. It is a willing, wanting, aching venture into the desert of our nature, loving the emptiness of that desert because of the sure knowledge that God's rain will fall and the certainty that we are both heirs and cocreators of the wonder that is now and of the Eden that is yet to be.[7]

This is the promise of simplicity. Not that we are giving up things just so we can call ourselves minimalists, but that we are giving up things to experience more of God. We are opening our hearts and hands to the love and wonder and hope and faithfulness that is the atmosphere of the presence of God. And restoration is the fruit of hearts that are once again awakened to the goodness of God. Restoration is the fruit of the Holy Spirit; the love and goodness and faithfulness and temperance and kindness that we are missing in the world is the fruit of pursuing God. When we find our joy in him, culture will be transformed, one home at a time.

> This is the promise of simplicity. Not that we are giving up things just so we can call ourselves minimalists, but that we are giving up things to experience more of God.

STUDY GUIDE

How have you embraced simplicity?

Was simplicity modeled in your home of origin?

How do you feel when your surroundings are cluttered?

Habits of Simplicity: Here are a few suggestions; feel free to add your own.

Limit screen time.   Keep a budget.

Limit shopping time.   Enjoy simple pleasures.

Track your time.   Use what you have.

What rule will you adopt in pursuit of simplicity? Examples:

The _____ family buys only what we need.

The _____ family gives away one item for every item we
      acquire.

Or write your own here:

_____

_____

When you have decided on your statement about habits of simplicity, you can plug it into the Your Family Rule template in the
appendix.

—— A VERSE TO MEMORIZE ——

Keep your life free from love of money, and be content with what you have, for he has said, "I will never leave you nor forsake you."

Hebrews 13:5

—— A PRAYER ——

Dear God, thank you for your generosity and provision. Thank you for my home and my family. Thank you for all the ways you have been good to me. I confess that I've used material possessions to mask unrest. Please teach me to simplify so that I can have more time for you and your people. I know that you are good and that you will give me all that I need.

—— FURTHER READING ——

The Pastor's Wife by Sabina Wurmbrand
Tortured for Christ by Richard Wurmbrand
Simply Living Well: A Guide to Creating a Natural, Low-Waste Home by Julia Watkins

A RECIPE TO TRY

Potato Latkes

4 large potatoes, grated
2 large eggs, lightly beaten
½ cup flour
1 teaspoon salt

⅓ cup olive oil
¼ cup finely chopped or grated onion

PREP: 30 minutes COOK: 30 minutes TOTAL: 60 minutes

1. Cover potatoes with water and a dash of salt; let rest for 15 minutes.

2. Beat together eggs, flour, salt, and olive oil.

3. Drain and rinse potatoes. Press excess water out with a clean towel.

4. Add grated potatoes and onion to beaten egg mixture.

5. Fry in hot coconut oil for 1–2 minutes per side.

6. Serve hot, topped with sour cream, plain yogurt, or applesauce.

Serves 4

7

HABITS OF STABILITY

Ruth Bell Graham

If our children have the background of a godly, happy home and this unshakeable faith that the Bible is indeed the Word of God, they will have a foundation that the forces of hell cannot shake.

Ruth Bell Graham

The setting of some of my first childhood memories is the Canadian farming community where my dad's family had lived since the early 1900s. My great-grandparents had emigrated to this sweeping Alberta prairie to build a new life for themselves, and my dad told stories of his childhood in the 1940s that sounded a lot like the stories Laura Ingalls Wilder told. His first home was a tar-paper claim shanty without electricity or indoor plumbing; the cold wind from below-zero temperatures would whistle through cracks in the walls, and my grandma cooked meals without the luxury of electric lights or refrigeration, which didn't come to their prairie home until the '50s.

By the time I arrived, the farm provided a comfortable living for my parents and grandparents. Our extended family went to the same church for years, enjoyed rowdy family reunions at the old one-room schoolhouse on the corner, where baseball games and tasty potlucks punctuated the summer months, and we spent Christmas with all our cousins, aunts, and uncles. In the summer, we could walk safely from Grandma's house to the candy store and the park, where we would spin wildly on the merry-go-round. The town was small, and we knew everyone. On the surface it was a sweet Mayberry-like life with roots that went deep.

But there was a dark side as well. When I was a five- or six-year-old child, wandering around on the family farm where I should have been safe, a friendly hired worker pulled me into a barn and molested me. An extended family member had porn hidden in their room, and we children discovered it one quiet afternoon and huddled around the curious sight of naked men. This destruction of innocence had consequences, and in extended play times when parents were distracted during fellowship with their friends, a boy stole one of the girl's clothes, and a few of us played a nasty game of doctor. It wasn't just the children who were misbehaving; the small community church also had a sinister element of control. The pastors were heavy handed about what church members did in their free time, how often they were at church, and on what they spent their money. As I mentioned earlier, when the church leaders discovered that my parents had the audacity to consider moving away, they tried to intimidate my dad into staying through threats and curses.

This was to be the straw that pushed my parents out of what seemed like such a safe community. We first landed in Oregon, where an aunt offered a home while my dad looked for work. We lived there among the ferns and moss for a few years, but in that coastal town where logging was being shut down, my farmer dad struggled to find steady employment. We ventured out again, this time arriving in bustling Sacramento, California, with its four-lane freeways and hot summers. It was overwhelming for myself and my four siblings, a completely different culture from the Canadian prairie and the Oregon coast. And, because of my parents' experience with the church in Canada, finding a church community was difficult.

This struggle to plug in and find a church community plagued all of us. My parents stayed in the greater Sacramento region; eventually all five of their children married there, and thirty-four grandchildren were added to their tribe. But while we became more geographically stable as a family (my sisters have lived in the same homes for over twenty years), we have all struggled to stay at one church. My husband and I are the nomads of the family, moving fifteen times in our thirty-three years of marriage, and in the six years in our peaceful mountain town, we've attended three different churches. We've also contemplated an out-of-state move for at least two of those six years. Needless to say, stability is not our natural strong point.

And why does stability matter for saving the world? How does stability have an impact on restoration? What is stability?

The Merriam-Webster dictionary definition sheds a little light:

> 1: the quality, state, or degree of being stable: such as
>   a: the strength to stand or endure : FIRMNESS
>   b: the property of a body that causes it when disturbed
>   from a condition of equilibrium or steady motion to
>   develop forces or moments that restore the original
>   condition
>   c: resistance to chemical change or to physical
>   disintegration
> 2: residence for life in one monastery[1]

Simply stated, stability is defined by the strength to endure, equilibrium, and resistance to physical disintegration. In the

Benedictine tradition, stability means that the monks make a vow to remain in the monastery they started in. They committed to stay where they were, no matter how they felt. The idea they held was that constantly moving around prevents us from becoming faithful to our calling. Saint Benedict writes that after a monk has joined and been received in the community, "from this day he is no longer free to leave the monastery."[2]

I can't imagine modern families taking a vow to stay in one place forever, or committing to one church or community for life. It seems extreme, but the Benedictines aren't the only ones who saw value in staying committed to one place. Wendell Berry is an author from Kentucky who believed in the virtue of stability. One author writes of Wendell Berry, "Berry has personified the monastic vow of stability. One place, one calling, one voice, one message, one wife, one family, one community, one home."[3]

Berry left the place where his family had farmed for generations and went to college to study English, followed by a few years living abroad and teaching in New York. In 1964, he returned to his hometown in Kentucky, bought a farm, and became a prolific advocate for loving the land and the people in your community, writing more than thirty books related to these subjects. He believed that saving the world started at home. It was done through simple acts such as loving your neighbors and caring for your land. He refined his prescription for saving the world into a list of ten values that include these statements:

- "Make a home. Help to make a community. Be loyal to what you have made."
- "Put the interest of the community first."
- "Love your neighbors—not the neighbors you pick out, but the ones you have."
- "As far as you are able, make your lives dependent upon your local place, neighborhood, and household—which

thrive by care and generosity—and independent of the industrial economy, which thrives by damage."

- "Find work, if you can, that does no damage. Enjoy your work. Work well."[4]

His thinking and his prescriptions might seem idealistic, but the potential for transforming a community when we live in one place long enough to care about it is profound.

Of course, some of us may need to move for a job or a missionary calling, and in the Bible there are several times when God told his people to go to a new place. Abraham was told to leave the home of his father, "Now the LORD had said to Abram: 'Get out of your country, from your family and from your father's house, to a land that I will show you' (Genesis 12:1 NKJV). He wasn't even given the security of knowing where he was going. Centuries later, when Jesus was a newborn, God told Joseph to leave and flee to Egypt. "Now when they had departed, behold, an angel of the Lord appeared to Joseph in a dream, saying, 'Arise, take the young Child and His mother, flee to Egypt, and stay there until I bring you word; for Herod will seek the young Child to destroy Him'" (Matthew 2:13 NKJV).

> The potential for transforming a community when we live in one place long enough to care about it is profound.

So in a world where we are led by the Holy Spirit, we may not have the comfort of staying in the same church and the same geographic location our whole lives. Since 2020, many families have relocated to be closer to family, or away from violent cities, or to states they felt were more accommodating to their family values. My family has been in the same uncomfortable limbo, concerned with some of the changes in our state and yet equally uneasy about leaving our home and community. We have the experience of several moves under our belts, so we know that transitions always have a cost. Our move to Mexico as missionaries helped us grow as a family, but also brought about marital difficulties. Our move to a different town in California for a job was the beginning of a hard and lonely season, but our family became closer as a result of it. Each move we make will create some friction, and it's important to be prayerful before making a big move.

A Stable Woman

Stability can be defined in more ways than staying in one community your whole life. Ruth Bell Graham was born in China to missionaries, and as she grew up, she hoped to return one day to serve the Lord. Her parents had left their Virginia home to serve in a Chinese hospital, but Ruth's childhood in China was interspersed with time in the United States, dodging danger as the country hurtled toward war. She was sent to boarding school in Korea for her high school years and spent her senior year of high school in Montreat, North Carolina, where her parents enjoyed a furlough. She was a young woman without a permanent place, and her childhood ambition was to go to another foreign field to be a missionary.

But what Ruth lacked in stability of location in childhood, she made up for with internal stability. While she was at Wheaton College, her dreams of being a missionary were shelved when she met Billy Graham. Billy was an evangelist who could make no promises of an easy life and who was clear about his expectations for a wife and mother. Marriage to him would mean giving up her dreams of missions, and it took a period of searching to make that leap. She wrote to her parents, "To be with Bill in this type of work won't be easy. There will be little financial backing, lots of obstacles and criticism, and no earthly glory whatsoever. But somehow I need Bill. I don't know what I'd do if, for some reason, he should suddenly go out of my life. And Bill needs someone to

116

understand him, someone who would be willing to take the quiet place of praying for him."[5]

For Ruth, stability evolved into creating a haven for her husband. While he traveled the world preaching the gospel to millions, she created a refuge nestled in the North Carolina mountains. In this small community she raised her children, taught Sunday school, and fed the poor. She lovingly designed a home in the mountains built from wood scrounged out of abandoned cabins, and learned to love her physical place in the world as well as her calling as a wife, mother, and leader. Billy Graham once lovingly described his wife's nature and partnership in his ministry: "Her disposition is the same all the time—very sweet and very gracious and charming. When it comes to spiritual things, my wife has had the greatest influence on my ministry."[6]

We live in a world where this kind of faithfulness, this ability to stay the course, is rarely seen. Instead, what's often encouraged today is summed up in shallow messages that promote emotional decisions, such as "Follow your heart," and "If it feels good, do it." Ruth Bell Graham didn't live with an entitled mindset—*My husband isn't meeting my emotional needs so I'm going to leave*; she lived with an eternal mindset. She was willing to give up her claim on her husband's time for the sake of the gospel. Her faithfulness allowed him to reach millions for the Lord, and her ability to stay steadfast and continue in prayer and joy even through loneliness is inspiring.

I've had a few short seasons when my own husband was gone for work or training, and my natural reaction was to want him to make it up to me. I wanted him to reward me for taking on the extra work while he was gone, even if his absence was directly beneficial to our family. But Matthew 24:13 (KJV) says, "But he that shall endure unto the end, the same shall be saved." One way we model stability is by being faithful to our marriage vows even when it isn't fun. We model world-changing stability by providing a safe and secure home for our children to grow up in, and by illustrating to them what commitment looks like.

Grit Equals Happiness

My parents modeled stability for their five children. They've been married for over fifty years, and while they have experienced hardship and loss, their steadfast faithfulness to each other has been a model for all of us to follow. When they lived on the farm in Canada, my mom would hang laundry outside in below-freezing temperatures to provide clean clothes for her family. When they lived in Oregon, they worked multiple jobs to provide food for their five children, and in California, my mom worked alongside my dad in his business. She wasn't afraid of work or difficulty and she raised her five children with the same pioneer spirit. My parents' stability meant that all five of their children stayed committed to their marriages, raised their own children with a strong sense of purpose and conviction, and contributed to local economies. Along with their thirty-four grandchildren, they have ten great-grandchildren who are being raised with the same sense of purpose and belief that they can make a difference in the world. The grandchildren have also seen their parents exhibit grit and stability in the way they overcome hardship and stay faithful to their families. We aren't a perfect family; we all make mistakes, but stability isn't a quest for perfection; it is a quest to stay the course even when it is hard. Psalm 37:3 (KJV) says, "Trust in the LORD, and do good; so shalt thou dwell in the land, and verily thou shalt be fed." Faithfulness means just doing your best each day to do the right thing even when it's hard. It's just another word for grit. And grit, according to Professor Angela Duckworth, is the greatest indicator for future happiness. She said, "Grit not only predicts objective measures of success, but it also predicts subjectively feeling happy, feeling a lot of positive emotion on a daily basis, and also feeling overall satisfied with your life."[7]

I'm sure that Ruth Bell Graham's faithfulness had an impact on her family as well. She raised five children, mostly without the presence of her husband. When I watched the funeral speeches for both Ruth and Billy, they revealed great depths of love from the children. In a post from the Billy Graham Evangelical Association, their daughter Gigi recounts, "Not once did my mother make us feel that by staying behind she was sacrificing her life for us children. By her sweet, positive example, her consistently unselfish spirit, and her total reliance upon the Person of Jesus Christ, we were kept from becoming bitter or resentful. Instead, we learned to look for ways to keep busy and prepare for Daddy's homecoming."[8]

But staying committed to a marriage isn't the only way to model stability. Sometimes our commitment to a marriage isn't enough to save it anyway. I have several friends who love God and his Word, who live with a high level of intentionality and commitment, and who generously care for their families, and yet their marriages still ended because we live in a fallen world. And while a cohesive marriage is a legacy for our children and our community, we can still live with commitment through the adverse circumstance of divorce. My friend Betsy wrote about the ending of her marriage:

> When my marriage of 20 years abruptly and unexpectedly came to a close, I found myself sitting in the rubble of a broken home. For my entire adult life I had been one half of a whole. I asked the Father if I could be whole on my own? Could I be strong enough to protect my children? The answer was: No. No! Gently, He showed me that this was never the burden I was created to bear. Only He could come in and fill in the cracks that this earth shaking event created in my family. Only He could bind up our wounds and set our feet once more on solid ground. While this season could have been one of anguish and fear, he turned it into one of renewal and hope. Did my children and I grieve? Yes, but we grieved as those who trust in his goodness. He led me to create new rhythms, while still honoring our family traditions. I found that I could not just continue our lives as before, with the empty place always before us. We had to sift through the rubble of our broken home and choose

what would create a new, strong foundation for our family. He stirred up a desire in us for adventure. While home continues to be a place of warmth, solace, and safety, we found that we craved fresh beauty, uncharted lands, and new memories to build our changing lives on. Prayers and hymns hold new meaning when they've been sung on the mountaintops as well as by the hearth. And wherever we go, our feet are always safe on the solid Rock.[9]

Maybe you are also in a season of upheaval and wondering how you can create stability for your children. Whether it is a move, a marriage ending, or simply the change of adding a new baby to the family, there are practical steps we can take to have inner calm as an anchor in a season of change.

1. **Anchor yourself in Christ.** The secret to Ruth Bell Graham's stability was not that her home in the mountains was in a safe and secure place; the secret was her daily dedication to time with God. We can never become stable people on our own, but when we regularly read the Word of God, meditate on the truth, and stay close to God, we can live out the steadfastness of God to our children in seasons of upheaval.

2. **Forgive.** I wrote extensively about this in *Mothering by the Book*, but holding on to grudges is the fastest path to instability and unreasonable behavior. The Bible says in Ephesians 4:26–27, "Do not let the sun go down on your anger, and give no opportunity to the devil." I've seen that when people hold on to hurts and let them fester, the result is erratic behaviors. Instead, be zealous about daily forgiving those who have trespassed against you. This doesn't mean you erase the consequences or stay in abusive relationships. It just means that you release them to God instead of carrying hatred and giving the enemy an opportunity to trouble you.

3. **Find godly counsel.** Sometimes we make big changes: leaving a church, moving to a different community, going to a new school, or ending a marriage, because we are in a painful season. Often, if we just stay where we are, the hardship will turn a corner and things will get better. However, if every time things get hard we jump ship, we just end up in a new hard place. I've seen families move to a new community only to find the new location even more difficult to plug into than the previous one. Some end a marriage and find that the next relationship is even more destructive. Even a change as simple as putting your kids back in school because you feel unhappy homeschooling (or the inverse) will lead to different hardships. So instead of just making those big changes, take time to get some godly counsel and pray so you make wise and thoughtful decisions.

4. **Practice thankfulness.** Many times, our instability is the result of not appreciating the good about the current situation. However, if we can learn to have eyes wide open to the joy of our lives now, it can help us avoid the pain of needless transition. Learn to love the home you are in, the community you are in, and the family God has given you by giving thanks for small blessings. As you learn to notice and love your life, you become a more settled person.

Even with all these ideas for developing stability, sometimes we suffer while we wait for circumstances to change. While I was working on this chapter, my husband was away at a ministry training. He would drive the four hours home each weekend to do home repairs, help our youngest son with his homework, and cook breakfast for the family before driving back on Sunday for his evening church service. Because our two youngest were taking co-op classes, it was taking us some time to join him. He still did his best to make it back to us each weekend and to stay connected during the week. Still, my attitude suffered. I felt alone and irritated, not sure we were doing the right thing. I chafed at the extra responsibilities that fell on me in his absence, and I shared my frustrations with him on more than a few occasions. I was no Ruth Bell Graham, so it was propitious that while I was experiencing this separation for a greater cause, I was reading about her life. I found myself wanting to be more like her. I wanted the courage and confidence to support my husband in his pursuit of God's calling instead of making his life harder by complaining about the hardships. Ruth wasn't insecure about her husband being gone, whining about not getting enough of his time and attention. According to her youngest son, Ned, "There is absolutely no insecurity in the woman. . . . There is total and absolute peace and confidence of who she is in God through Christ."[10]

This word picture of the gracious way Ruth Bell Graham managed the separation from her husband meant so much to me. I wanted to be confident and serene so that despite the upheaval and chaos in the world around me, I could create stability simply through my own internal peace. Ruth Bell Graham had the peace of God—wherever she was, she carried that peace.

There are many ways we can demonstrate world-saving stability. It might be as simple as sticking to one habit for a time while you build the muscle of self-control. It might mean that you continue at the same school or homeschool co-op for a season. It might be just the consistency of putting dinner on the table every night that brings a sense of stability and peace in your home. We may not be making a vow to stay in the same church for life like the Benedictine monks or adopting Wendell Berry's philosophy of living on the same piece of land forever, but when we learn to be anchored in Christ and steadfast in our commitments, stability is the natural and world-changing fruit of our efforts.

STUDY GUIDE

Would you describe your childhood as stable?

Who has modeled stability for you?

How have you struggled with stability?

Habits of Stability: Pick a few habits to work on and add to your family rule of life.

> Keep family routines.
> Establish traditions.
> Stay in the same church, school, or home.
> Be faithful in relationships.
> Practice thankfulness.
> Be faithful in studying the Word of God.

What rule will you adopt? For example:

The _____ family practices thankfulness.
The _____ family reads the Bible every day.

Or write your own here:

_____

_____

When you have decided on your statement about habits of stability, you can plug it into the Your Family Rule template in the appendix.

——— A VERSE TO MEMORIZE ———

Therefore, my beloved brothers, be steadfast, immovable, always abounding in the work of the Lord, knowing that in the Lord your labor is not in vain.

1 Corinthians 15:58

——— A PRAYER ———

God, thank you for being the Rock of our salvation. Thank you for your steadfast love. Forgive me for the ways I have tried to create stability in my own strength. Forgive me for the ways I have been inconsistent and chaotic in my daily decisions. Please help me to stay anchored in you so that I can create a safe haven for my family, no matter where you place us.

——— FURTHER READING ———

A Time for Remembering: The Story of Ruth Bell Graham by Patricia Daniels Cornwell
Footprints of a Pilgrim by Ruth Bell Graham
Hannah Coulter by Wendell Berry

A RECIPE TO TRY

Biscuits and Gravy

PREP: 20 minutes COOK: 25 minutes TOTAL: 45 minutes

For the biscuits:

2 cups all-purpose flour	1 teaspoon salt
1 teaspoon baking powder	8 tablespoons butter
1 teaspoon sugar	1 cup buttermilk

1. Heat oven to 425° F.

2. Mix flour, baking powder, sugar, and salt in a food processor.

3. Add butter and pulse until butter is mostly mixed in.

4. Add buttermilk and barely mix. The key to light biscuits is to avoid over-mixing.

5. Drop batter by tablespoons on a cookie sheet. Pat down lightly.

6. Bake for 10–12 minutes.

For the Gravy:

1 package ground pork sausage	2½ cups milk
¼ cup flour	Salt

1. Cook biscuits according to recipe or package ingredients.

2. Cook sausage in a heavy skillet over medium heat until thoroughly cooked.

3. Stir flour into cooked sausage and pan drippings.

4. Gradually add milk, stirring constantly with a whisk or fork until gravy is thickened.

5. Reduce heat to medium low and add salt and pepper to taste.

6. To serve, split biscuits in half and spoon ⅛ to ¼ cup gravy over each biscuit half.

Serves 6

8

HABITS OF HOSPITALITY

Ella "Mama" Tweten

It is not what you have that is important. . . . It is what you believe. God never fails. That we believe!

Ella Tweten in *First We Have Coffee* by Margaret Jensen

It was a late summer weekend, and our home was bursting at the seams. All of our six young (at the time) children were sleeping on the floor or a chair or squeezed into the bed with us in our bedroom, while the other bedrooms in the house were occupied by my sister's family and twenty of their best church friends. We were missionaries, living on a barren coastal hillside in Mexico just a mile from a huge housing development that sprawled out of Tijuana. If we looked to the west, we could see a few houses near a golf course, a few horses in a pasture, and a small brick-making operation. Beyond that lay the blue waters of the Pacific Ocean. Behind our home rose a hillside, a dirt field in dry seasons but a yellow field of wildflowers when the rain came. However, as you drove just over the hill to the east, you entered another world. It was a loud, wild place with horns beeping, pedestrians walking to bus stops, and brightly colored signs lining the roadside advertising everything from pizza to laundry soap. Our home just on the other side of the hill was a sweet, quiet refuge after a long day of service.

The church group was there to build a bathroom for an underfunded orphanage. A local couple had been caring for nineteen children in a small house with only one bathroom. The floor under the bathtub had rotted out, and the tub was sitting at an angle as it pushed through to the ground beneath. The boys at the home slept on bare mattresses in the living room, which they stacked against the wall during the daytime, and the girls and parents were squeezed into the other two rooms. During the day, our houseful of American families would head to the orphanage to build, while at night we all squeezed back into our home for dinner, hoping the weather would allow for outdoor eating. The guests all helped with the meals, and it was a joy to gather around the table for pasta and garlic bread while we recapped the events of the day, or to sip coffee together in the morning while watching the fog roll off the coastline.

Hospitality has always been a part of our family culture. When I was a new bride, I hosted my parents for dinner, serving them burnt spaghetti, a calamity I can hardly comprehend hundreds of spaghetti dinners later. For our first Christmas as a married couple, I held a party in our small apartment; guests brought ornaments to decorate our barren tree, and I served appetizers (none of them burnt!). We continued this tradition of hospitality as our family grew, hosting ladies' Bible studies, small groups, baby showers, and barbecues. We weren't afraid to host strangers either. One moonless night a car pulled down our isolated country driveway, and a group of four young people stepped out. They were Czechoslovakian tourists looking for a campground. They asked about camping in our field, but instead we offered them the use of our detached schoolroom. After they set up their sleeping bags, we gathered around our dining table for a halting conversation, the language barrier standing in the way of real understanding. In the morning they drove away, leaving miniature bottles of spirits from their home country as a parting gift.

But hosting family groups at our home in Mexico was a whole new adventure. We wanted families to get a taste of what missions were like and learn to simplify their lives for a higher purpose after seeing the poverty on display there. We were excited to have strangers come stay in our home with us so they could give their children this life-changing experience. And I was honestly super happy for the company. Even though these groups arrived as strangers, I was living as an extrovert in a country where I didn't speak the language, so I was delighted to have English speakers in my home.

And showing hospitality to strangers is an integral part of the biblical account. In Genesis 18, Abraham is sitting in the door of his tent and sees three men. He instantly understands the importance of this visit and fetches water to wash their feet, hurrying to have fine cakes and meat prepared to feed them. His enthusiastic hospitality was timely, for it turned out to be a heavenly visitation of angels. I think we'd all rush to prepare food if the Lord himself were visiting. But we aren't called only to roll out the red carpet for Jesus. In the New Testament we are admonished to entertain strangers, because in caring for and serving others, we serve and show love to Jesus.

Hospitality Restores

Hospitality was another way the Benedictines saved culture and civilization during the fall of the Roman Empire. They didn't have a completely closed-off way of life; their prayers, work, order, and balance were on display. Strangers were always welcome, and as the doors were opened to them, people were able to experience the peace and presence of God. They could see the contrast between the chaos of the world and the serenity of this set-apart place. In Rule 53 Saint Benedict writes that all guests "are to be welcomed as Christ," noting that Jesus himself would say, "I was a stranger and you welcomed me" (Matthew 25:35), and urging that honor be shown to everyone, especially to fellow Christians, "those who are of the household faith" (Galatians 6:10), as well as to pilgrims.[1]

Hospitality is of high importance to God. On the day of judgment, one of the qualifiers of whether we really knew him or not is if we welcomed strangers. Paul puts it directly in Romans 12:13, telling us to "practice hospitality," and then finishes the chapter with an exhortation to go so far as to feed our enemy. Hospitality, whether it's cheese and crackers or the full Thanksgiving dinner, is how we get past mere surface relationships. Hospitality is how communion happens, and it's how we build a community. When we break bread with people around a table, we come to know people and they come to know us; this is how we save the world.

> Hospitality is how communion happens, and it's how we build a community. When we break bread with people around a table, we come to know people and they come to know us; this is how we save the world.

If we spend our days alone with the doors closed to others, then the special way of life we are cultivating becomes only a stagnant pond. In order to be fresh, sweet water, there needs to be an inflow and an outflow. As we learn from the Lord, as we read the Word together and pray, as we look each other in the eyes and smile, as we live lives full of peace and joy because the Lord is teaching us, we must open the doors so that others can experience this peace as well. Hospitality is a command because aside from performing a miracle, it's the best way to reach a broken world. People see the gospel in action when we open our homes, especially as the world grows darker. And while turning water into wine or raising the dead are the miraculous ways Jesus showed the goodness of God to a broken world, when we sit together for a meal without our phones distracting us, or when we respond kindly to each other, it is a miracle. In an era when many people have lost the ability to converse, and fear of repeating their parents' mistakes has left many childless and alone, to have someone invite you into a family is miraculous.

Ella Tweten was one such miracle worker in the 1930s. She was the wife of a Norwegian pastor, and in her early days of marriage she had experienced great loss as diphtheria took the life of her two-year-old daughter. Instead of isolating herself, she took her despair to God and received his comfort. Thus encouraged, she was able to open her heart and home to others. While she held down the home on the Canadian prairie, her husband traveled to minister to immigrants, and she offered the warmth of her table to the lonely. Her daughter Margaret Jensen, who authored Ella Tweten's biography, *First We Have Coffee*, recounts the discomfort she felt when her mother hosted a depressed immigrant who often stopped by Ella's kitchen for a bite to eat.

> He spoke seldom, but stared into space—and drank coffee. Mama said he was very sick on the inside. He had left the big woods to work in a factory, trying to save money to bring his wife from Norway.
>
> I had only one complaint of his frequent visits. "But, Mama, his feet smell so bad! Can't you do something?"[2]

Ella Tweten ran an open home, and the depressed, lonely, and smelly were welcome there. Upon her daughter's suggestion, she began offering a warm tub of water for the man to soak his feet in, while she furtively washed and dried his socks. Each week, he soaked his feet and picked up a bundle of clean clothes. Ella's simple acts of love created the atmosphere for hope.

Gradually the dazed look of shock disappeared. As he drank coffee, Mama's guitar music seemed to seep into his thoughts and replace some of his pain. One day he burst into the kitchen, exploding with joy! "My Hilda comes! My Hilda comes!" That ended the foot washing ceremony in Mama's kitchen.[3]

Mama's hospitality to a rancid, homesick man gave him the will to work and to earn enough to send for his beloved. The kindness of this family saved him. The book tells of countless moments when hospitality created hope that helped people recover from the shock and loneliness of being in a new land. It also tells of the miraculous hospitality they themselves experienced. Once, they were driving across the Saskatchewan prairie toward their new home. Lunch was gone, their money was gone, and Mama wistfully said how much she would love a cup of coffee and a bowl of soup. In an effort to please her, Papa stopped at the first house he saw and proceeded to ask for a cup of coffee. The owner of the simple white cottage invited them in and served them an entire meal. They thanked him as they left and promised to repay the kindness. Later, when Papa returned to repay the man, there was no house, and no man. Papa asked around the community and was told that no such house had ever been there. Margaret Jensen wrote of the incident, "I was humbled, thinking this must have been one of God's rewards to Mama and Papa, who so freely served 'angels unaware.'"[4]

In a small way, I could relate to some of the sacrifices they had made. When we lived in Mexico and hosted families for missionary experiences, hardship was involved. We had to conserve water because our off-grid home was dependent on a single tanker truck of water each week. That one thousand gallons of water ran out quickly, and the truck wasn't always available to deliver more. Cooking for a group involved hours spent on my feet while pregnant, and we also had a guest with smelly feet to endure. I wish I had thought to let him soak his feet in a bowl of water, because our eyes burned with the acrid smell as soon as his shoes were off.

But my discomforts were small compared with what it cost Mama Tweten, on a meager pastor's salary, to provide for guests. Reading her biography, I was awed by her generosity and faithfulness. She created an atmosphere that drew people in despite the hardships she faced, even the hardship of a somewhat insensitive husband. When they moved to Brooklyn to pastor a church, she continued to welcome strangers into her home, including forty-five children for whom she cared as the administrator of a children's home. When most women would have chosen a leisurely life after their children were grown, she took on the care of many more children. Her devotion to God was evident in her love for others, and it brought restoration to her home and countless others. One of the boys from the children's home recounts the first night Mama Tweten came to their dormitory, her time with them an experience he credits with keeping the boys from winding up in reform school:

> We had planned some bold adventures and waited for her to make her rounds. Instead, she sat down on Bob's bed, sang Norwegian songs and read the Bible and prayed for each one of us by name . . . kissed us all good night and told us she loved us . . . said, "God bless you, *my* boys." We couldn't carry out our plans.[5]

Hospitality in a restoration home does have its boundaries, however. While we are to be ready to entertain strangers, there is also the command to bring children up "in the nurture and admonition of the Lord" (Ephesians 6:4 KJV), and this requires thoughtfulness in the welcoming of guests. It requires having already established some order and daily practices so that we keep the boat in the water, without letting the water get in the boat, especially in terms of impressionable children and guests whose values don't reflect our own. But the truth is, most of the bad influences on our children are not from worldly guests, but rather from the media we consume; if our family is grounded in the Word of God and being thoughtful about what we watch and listen to, hosting an atheist for dinner isn't likely to undermine our faith.

But how do we keep up the healthy routines and order we have established while also welcoming guests? Prolific hosts like Mama Tweten can help guide us. Just as Mama Tweten hosted lonely Norwegian immigrants during the Great Depression era, Corrie ten Boom "hosted" Jewish families in World War II Holland, helping them hide from the Nazis. In both cases, the family routines stayed the same, even with extra people around. They still read the Bible in the morning. They still did the work that was at hand. Instead of making a big deal about guests and trying to have the house perfectly clean and a five-course meal prepared, they simply folded new people into the activity of the home, being careful to protect sacred rhythms of work and rest. In *Seeking God*, Esther de Waal writes how the Benedictines did this as well:

> The cheerful greeting is right and St. Benedict is insistent that the porter is always ready with his warm response. The ritual of the kiss of peace and the sharing of food has its modern counterpart. But this most genuine and loving reception is balanced by a very serious attention on the part of the Rule to the vital importance of protecting the peace and silence of the monastery against any intrusion that might unduly disturb its order. St. Benedict is careful to impose limits so that the life and work of the monastery can go on.[6]

Healthy Rhythms Are Key

While welcoming strangers is an important Christian virtue that can change the world and bring restoration, healthy rhythms are key so that children don't get lost in the shuffle. Strong parent-child attachment is important for their well-being, daily spiritual rhythms are important for their soul, and it takes much care to balance parenting with hospitality. When we hosted people in our home in Mexico, the entire time was busy, with connection hard to come by. My children played with any visiting kids, and we would briefly exchange a hug and a prayer at bedtime, or I would try to gather them close during group devotions. But when the group left, we had a family debrief time, and I loved it. We would cuddle on the couch and talk about our impressions of the weekend, our highlights, and what meant the most to us. It was a chance to share our hearts and to reconnect after the hustle of hosting.

We also took time after hosting to talk about any issues that came up for my children. In my own childhood, unsupervised playtime opened the door to shame and trauma as our conversations and behavior veered into danger zones. Instead of leaving my children to themselves with strangers around, I was intentional about checking in on them while we had a houseful of people. When the guests had all left, we made sure to talk about any issues that had come up and say a prayer of blessing for the travelers and a prayer of cleansing over our home. One morning stands out in my memory of confusing issues. The adults were in the house praying for the day, and the guys had the unpleasant task ahead of them to recover one of our guests' stolen cars. A visit to the Tijuana police station was their first stop. We prayed quietly, listening to the chatter of the children, but then in the middle of the prayer, we heard my five-year-old yell, "You go to hell!"

What we hadn't heard was the preceding conversation between these two mini theologians. One was arguing that hell was not real, and my own dear child was trying to explain that hell was a literal place where sinners go. What we also didn't hear were the clarifiers, "You do too go to hell," as in that is the destination of sinners in general, but not that child in particular. So after the group left, we had a conversation about theology, and about not arguing with guests even if we disagree with them (or at least not with raised voices while the adults are praying). We returned to our quiet daily rhythms of prayer and homeschooling, thankful for the gift of guests but also for the gift of quiet.

And hospitality doesn't only serve others. When we open the door to neighbors and friends, even if it's just a weekly rhythm, it gives people a chance to know us and love us. We have one neighbor who brings us delicious organic fruit weekly throughout summer, and a previous neighbor shared her fragrant citrus with us, becoming an adopted grandma to my children. We've been blessed by the love of our neighbors, and Mama Tweten was the recipient of neighborly love as well. In *First We Have Coffee*, her daughter tells of a Christmas when their father was away doing ministry, and the cupboards were bare. Her mother prayed for provision and sat down with the children to wait on God. She told her children, "We are well. We are not hungry. We are warm. We have oatmeal, a little coffee—and sugar lumps. Papa is in God's service and God takes care of His children."[7]

Suddenly there was a knock at the door and a shout of happy voices. In poured boxes of food and gifts straight from the generous hearts of the First Baptist Church of Saskatoon. They had heard that Pastor Tweten was not yet back from his journey and came to bless the family. They sang and prayed together and then they left, with an invitation to Christmas dinner at the pastor's home. The hospitality Mama Tweten had shown to countless people was not unseen by God, and God takes care of his children.

Open Your Doors

Often, we hesitate to show hospitality because our homes aren't well-run little monasteries but rather a dumping ground in between activities where laundry litters the floor and the kitchen sink is full of dirty dishes. There are seasons in our lives when despite our best efforts, a certain amount of chaos is inevitable. In the season with small children, it can be hard just to get food on the table, not to mention cleaning it up. When my third child was born, my husband was working sixteen-hour days and coming home after dark, hungry and tired. He wasn't able to help me feed and bathe the children or clean up the kitchen. It was all on my shoulders, which meant the house wasn't always as clean as I wished. Sometimes people came over when there were dirty dishes in the sink or laundry on the couch. But opening our homes, regardless of their state, is what turns neighbors into friends and friends into family. In *Habits of the Household*, Justin Whitmel Earley writes of this same experience,

> Seeing with the liturgical lens expands our field of vision to see that the spiritually significant work of the household is not happening in spite of the mess but because of it. It also expands our field of vision to see that the work of the family is about more than the family.
>
> . . . we care for the family because it is through the household that God's blessing to us is extended to others.[8]

So open your doors. Set a goal to invite one person over every week, even if just for coffee or tea. Take a small step toward the practice of hospitality. Here are a few simple ideas to get you started.

Book Club—Gather a few friends or acquaintances to study a book together. Take one chapter a week and rotate homes so everyone gets a chance to practice hospitality. You can think of questions on your own for the book of choice or use one like this one that has included study questions and challenges.

Seasonal Parties—I loved hosting a spring party where children could dye hard-boiled eggs, hunt for chocolate eggs in the grass, and make nests in the trees. It was an outdoor party, which meant my home stayed a little cleaner, but it was fun to gather a group and connect with them. We also have hosted or attended gatherings such as a Christmas cookie exchange, ornament exchange, white-elephant gift exchange, Passover seder, Saint Patrick's Day dinner, Super Bowl parties, and more. Seasonal parties like these are often potluck-style or just require bringing an appetizer, which makes them more manageable for busy families.

Standing Dinners—Some people have a standing dinner date with adult children or friends and gather every week. Having a routine like this can take the pressure off trying to fit hospitality into an already busy schedule and be a comforting opportunity to be with people you love.

Coffee Dates—The simplest of gatherings is just inviting a friend over for coffee or tea. It doesn't require elaborate preparations to offer a cup of something hot in winter and cool in summer (bonus points if you have a baked good to accompany it—even if it wasn't baked by you!). Opening your home is a sacred invitation to enter your personal space, and it can fast-track deeper friendships when you allow someone in.

Impromptu Gatherings—We live in a different town than some of my extended family and my adult children, and there are often times when a visit from them is planned at the last minute, or there are those times when dinner is already cooking and a neighbor stops by, and you invite them to stay and eat with you. I think these are the best because you are relieved from the pressure of preparation, there is no chance to overthink what to serve or how tidy your home is, and you just get to enjoy the deepening friendship.

Worship and Communion—One of our favorite gatherings is a simple worship night in our backyard or living room. There is nothing so sweet as having our home bathed in prayer and offering fellowship around our mutual love of Jesus. True, there isn't a church janitor to clean up after people leave, but when you develop a community around adoration of Jesus, our homes are transformed into sanctuaries.

A few months into COVID, when we had a clearer idea of what the dangers were and were also desperately missing gathering with other believers, we hosted a worship night in our backyard. Nearly forty people gathered to sing to Jesus and take Communion together, and it held new meaning for all of us. Living in California with strict isolation policies, there was a real threat that police might show up at our door to shut us down, and as we worshiped, we had an opportunity to consider the persecuted church around the world. Suddenly, hospitality took on a new meaning as we reflected on the necessity of "not forsaking the assembling of ourselves" (Hebrews 10:25 KJV) during a crisis. This wasn't a casual dinner with friends or a festive holiday party. This was desperate soul care, civil disobedience for the sake of the cross.

Corrie ten Boom (who also exemplified community building, as we will see in chapter 9) knew this struggle well. Her family were law-abiding people, model citizens, and yet when she was faced with the decision to obey local authorities or open her doors to the Jews, she chose the path of true peace. Her home became a refuge, but regular showing of hospitality had already been a habit for her family. They were devoted to God and to loving people for God's sake, so the next step was an obvious one.

I'm not trying to compare hosting a worship night in my backyard during COVID in California to the heroism of Corrie ten Boom, but heroism does sometimes involve small, seemingly insignificant lifestyle changes, and hospitality is one way to let our light shine. In a time when families are rarely together, it's a life-saving experience when people get to see moms and dads and children loving each other and enjoying each other's company. When you invite people in, you are truly changing the world and opening up a vision for a loving family to those outside your four walls. Through witnessing the life and love of other families, we were shaped in our own journey as a family. Small habits like teaching our children to be respectful and considerate of adults were built because of what we saw other families doing, and big decisions like home-educating our children came as the result of what we saw when we were guests in another home.

This is still happening today. How many life decisions have you made because of what you witnessed in the lives of those around you? Restoration happens not just because we live according to the Word of God, or according to a biblical rule, but also because outsiders see our way of life and want to know the love of God as well. As believers, we have the hope of God, we have fellowship with God, and because of this we can have peace in any storm. When your best friend is the King of Kings, it changes everything. In his book *Praying Like Monks, Living Like Fools*, Tyler Staton writes,

> Monks of various traditions are instructed to picture the face of Jesus as they pray. It's an anchor, a point where their prayers always must return. We come with our requests, but it's him we are really seeking. We want to see him face-to-face. And in the face of Christ, we discover the hospitality of God.[9]

Hospitality is just inviting people into experiencing the love of God with us. The hospitable life of Mama Tweten might have seemed ordinary to her. The daily practices she kept, the regular prayer and mealtimes, and the open door she created were just a part of her normal, everyday life, but lives were changed as she opened her doors. When we open our homes, even homes with dirty laundry, dirty dishes in the sink, and crying babies, we are opening the doors of our sanctuary. And when we have made Jesus our lover and our friend, his love becomes part of the atmosphere. Amid the imperfection there exists the Spirit of God, and people encounter this love and are changed forever. Restoration happens one table at a time.

STUDY GUIDE

What does the Bible say about hospitality?

What makes hospitality hard for you?

What were your childhood experiences with hospitality?

Habits of Hospitality: Pick a few to add to your family rule or brainstorm your own.

Teach children to be kind to guests.

Keep an open home.

Keep a tidy guest bathroom.

Have easy snacks, coffee, or tea on hand.

Make a hosting routine.

What rule will your family adopt regarding hospitality? Some examples:

The _____ family will invite a friend for dinner every Friday.

The _____ family is hospitable to strangers.

Or write your own here:

_____

_____

When you have decided on your statement about habits of hospitality, you can plug it into the Your Rule of Life template in the appendix.

——— A VERSE TO MEMORIZE ———

Do not neglect to show hospitality to strangers, for thereby some have entertained angels unawares.

Hebrews 13:2

——— A PRAYER ———

Dear God, thank you that you created people to love and to be loved. Forgive me for the ways I have neglected to open my home and show hospitality. Help me to order my days in such a way that I can love your people well while still keeping time with you and my own family as the priority.

——— FURTHER READING ———

First We Have Coffee by Margaret Jensen
Habits of the Household by Justin Whitmel Earley
The Hiding Place by Corrie ten Boom
Teatime Discipleship by Sally Clarkson

A RECIPE TO TRY

Apple Crisp

5 large apples (we like golden delicious)
lemon juice
1 cup rolled oats
¾ cup brown sugar

½ cup flour (gluten-free works fine)
½ teaspoon salt
1 teaspoon cinnamon
½ cup softened butter

PREP: 20 minutes COOK: 45 minutes TOTAL: 65 minutes

1. Preheat the oven to 350° F.

2. Peel, core, and slice apples, and place in a pie plate.

3. Sprinkle a teaspoon or two of lemon juice on the apples and stir, to prevent browning.

4. Mix oats, brown sugar, flour, salt, and cinnamon, then stir or cut in butter.

5. Distribute over sliced apples and bake at 350° F for 45 minutes.

6. Serve warm with whipped cream.

Serves 6

9

HABITS OF COMMUNITY

Esther Jungreis

Because my father found the courage to hide those dry morsels for Shabbos, because of that, the bread made from sawdust became challah, and we understood that there was a higher purpose to our lives.

—Rebbetzin Esther Jungreis, *The Committed Life*

The bonfire blazed hot and bright as we sat around it singing to the gentle strum of guitar. It was October 31, and while many families enjoy a different tradition, for several years ours had been to worship with our community. One of the dads led us in Communion, we took time to pray, and then spent the whole evening singing praises to God while the children made copious amounts of hot cocoa at the nearby snack table. We were a broken bunch that night, weary from heavy circumstances: For one mama it was a hard homeschool day, for another family it was job transitions, and for myself, an afternoon spent fighting with a child over their co-op homework was worrying me and robbing me of joy. Our praise was indeed a sacrifice, a heartfelt offering to God from an empty well. But we were there because we loved each other. We had gone through intense turmoil as a community in the past, with broken relationships after a church split, but we had come through the fire with a commitment to God that was pure gold.

Many of the moves we have made as a family landed us in lonely places where we stuck out like a sore thumb. When we moved to Mexico, we didn't even fit in with the other missionaries. Most of them were retirees or ex-convicts without children to care for, but while it was uncomfortable to be on a lonely road, it did help us to learn to love and appreciate people who were doing life differently than we were.

When we moved to another new town for my husband's next job, we were once again on the outskirts of the community we found there. This time, however, it was our lifestyle that was different. We were living on a five-acre farm with fruit trees, a huge garden, and animals to care for, while most of our friends lived in suburban houses with small yards. Instead of wrestling baby goats for fun, they played video games. Instead of canning peaches in the middle of the hot summer, they went to amusement parks. Our lives weren't better or worse than theirs, just different, and sometimes differences can make us feel alone, or even wanting to change to fit in.

But while it was good for us to break out of a judgmental attitude and learn to appreciate people who are different from us, when we adjust our belief systems for the worse to accommodate our community, or when we change our behavior to fit in, problems follow. The Christian church as a whole has struggled with this over the years, and now for many there is confusion over what is right and what is wrong. Without a cohesive Christian community, there is seemingly no standard of Christian behavior. Where at one time there might have been social pressure to live according to biblical values, there is no such consensus now, and from church to church you can find a wild variation of interpretation of right and wrong, and often a dismissal of Scripture itself.

Creating Cohesive Communities

We may be confused about what standard to follow, but we aren't alone in our hunger to discover the way of life, how to keep our children safe from worldly influences, and what will make our homes a light for Jesus. We are especially anxious to find a true path because there are so many modern dilemmas we face that aren't specifically spelled out in Scripture. When the Israelites were in a similar situation, God spoke to them and said, "Thus says the Lord: Stand by the roads, and look, and ask for the ancient paths, where the good way is; and walk in it, and find rest for your souls" (Jeremiah 6:16).

The Benedictines are one group who have kept to an ancient path, but we've already established that joining a monastery is not a good solution for us, since our husbands and children rely on us to shape the home. Still, there are others who have developed a cohesive community and kept their values over the millennia. Corrie ten Boom is one Christian woman who was raised in a family and lived in a community that was so dedicated to their beliefs that they risked death to be true to a set of values God had laid on their hearts. While many Christians in Europe sat back and let the Holocaust happen, Corrie's family and friends had such a dedication to the Word of God that the just path of protecting the innocent became an imperative, despite the threat of prison camp. When they knew it soon would be discovered that they were hiding Jews, still they pressed on. In *The Hiding Place*, Corrie's story of her life, she writes,

> Once again we considered stopping the work. Once again we discovered we could not.

That night Father and Betsie and I prayed long after the others had gone to bed. We knew that in spite of daily mounting risks we had no choice but to move forward. This was evil's hour: we could not run away from it.[1]

Corrie gives insight to the foundation of such conviction, the practices of faith, family, and community that had hidden the Word of God in their hearts—habits that, despite all the external forces at work, didn't stop after they were arrested and being detained:

A group had gathered around father for evening prayers. Every day of my life had ended like this: that deep steady voice, that sure and eager confiding of us all to the care of God. The Bible lay at home on its shelf, but much of it was stored in his heart. His blue eyes seemed to be seeing beyond the locked and crowded room, beyond Haarlem, beyond earth itself, as he quoted from memory: "Thou art my hiding place and my shield: I hope in thy word. . . . Hold thou me up, and I shall be safe. . . ."[2]

Even when Corrie and her sister were suffering through the horrors of a German prison camp, they still formed a community around the Word of God. She writes, "As for us, from morning until lights-out, whenever we were not in ranks for roll call, our Bible was the center of an ever-widening circle of help and hope. The blacker the night around us grew, the brighter and truer and more beautiful burned the word of God."[3]

It's easy to look at Corrie and think she was able to live with this kind of dedication to sacred habits because she didn't have her own children to raise, or because she was living in wartime, which clarified values through the fire of persecution. But there is another exemplary woman, who lived among the hedonists of New York after World War II, and while not a believer in Jesus, still loved God's Word enough to form a community around it. Esther Jungreis was a Hungarian Jew whose family barely escaped extermination by the Nazis. Born in 1936, she was on a cattle car bound for Auschwitz with her parents and siblings when a relative with connections was able to get them transferred to a train bound for Switzerland. They were narrowly saved from the gas chambers with the help of family. The train did make a stop at the Bergen-Belsen concentration camp, and for six months she was interned there along with her family. After the war, they settled in Brooklyn, New York, with thousands of other Jewish refugees, where she began a ministry to Jews, urging them to keep the old paths of their ancestors. A *New York Times* article about her said, "Her style was impassioned, her message urgent. She routinely called the threat of assimilation 'a spiritual Holocaust.' Onstage, she would exhort and scold, admonish and warn, tugging at the heartstrings with both hands, distraught at the erosion of Jewish identity and religious devotion."[4]

She was driven to protect the Jewish community from losing their values through assimilation into American culture because she had seen the sacrifices her own parents had made in their devotion to God. While they were housed among the rats and lice of Bergen-Belsen, her father would set aside a few crumbs from his daily allowance of bread so that he could have a special Sabbath meal with his children. She writes of her father, "Because my father found the courage to hide those dry morsels for Shabbos, because of that, the bread made from sawdust became challah, and we understood that there was a higher purpose to our lives."[5]

Her father was willing to suffer for his faith, and it inspired his family to build a life that kept the rules of their faith. Instead of simply assimilating into the relative luxury and decadence of post–World War II New York, Esther urged her community to dedicate themselves to study of the Torah and to keep the practices that Jews had followed since the days of Moses. She urged people not to leave behind their values but instead to live a life committed to the teachings found in the Word. She said, "Our homes lack stability and serenity. Divorce and dysfunctional families have become the norm, and our schools are, at best, gateways to economic opportunity, preparing our children for careers and jobs but not for life. Our world is an angry world, high on bitterness and entitlement and low on kindness and generosity."[6]

The formula she gave to overcome these societal ills (which some would say have only grown worse in the years since she wrote) was deeds and action. Instead of being led by emotions, she believed in simply doing the next right thing and obeying God's Word with fidelity and care. She writes,

> If we harbor resentment against our parents, we must force ourselves to relate to them with respect. If we're not in the mood to pray, we must force ourselves to open the prayer book and pronounce those sacred words. The examples are endless, but if we stay with it, if we force ourselves to live by the discipline of G-d we will be able to tap into that pure source and become the person that G-d meant us to be.[7]

This is a revolutionary idea for many. We've been so used to following our emotions that the idea of doing something that doesn't sound fun is difficult. And for many Christians, myself included, the assurance of salvation can make us lazy about good works. For groups like Orthodox Jews and the Amish, their entry to heaven is to some degree predicated on their behavior here; they have the fear of the afterlife to keep them doing the right thing even when they don't feel like it. However, believers like myself, who rely solely on the shed blood of Jesus to save, can become careless about behavior, since we know that it's not our works that bring salvation. Still, knowing that Jesus has paid it all should fill us with love that motivates obedience to his Word, not with carelessness. It's hard to discern when we live with so many gray areas; sometimes we don't even know what is right or wrong. It can be confusing to figure out what Christians are supposed to do. Some churches interpret Scripture so differently, and modern society keeps pushing the envelope of what is morally acceptable. Many have lost the anchors that helped us stay on the path.

Esther Jungreis may not have had the comfort of knowing her sins were forgiven because of Jesus' death on the cross, but she valued the words of God she did have enough to take them seriously. Actions like telling the truth, avoiding gossip, and honoring your marriage vows were clearly extolled in the teachings, so she had no compunction about urging the virtue of obedience to Scripture in modern New York as well. Despite the bustling city they lived in, her family still halted everything on Friday evening to celebrate the Sabbath, because keeping the Sabbath was one of the basic rules of life they lived by. They didn't let their own values get swept away by the values of their new country, but instead formed a community around what was important to them and stayed steadfast to their faith. They lived out Deuteronomy 6, teaching the words of God to their own children as well as to their spiritual community.

Many of you are also forming communities around what is important to you. You are finding people who share similar values and who can help you create islands of civility in a world of chaos. Many of you gather regularly with your community to break bread, pray, and find support for your countercultural lifestyle. In my small community, we make soap together and process chickens for the freezer. We swap gardening advice and flower seeds. We share teaching duties in our homeschool co-op, hold worship nights, and offer accountability and counsel when we are going through a rough time. We gather for book clubs where we read books like *For the Family's Sake* by Susan Schaeffer Macauley to help us learn how to live as Christians today, in the world but not of the world. We are committed to our families and to God and we are supporting each other on that journey. We are attempting to be like Daniel, who stayed faithful to God even while living under Babylonian rule, or like Benedict, who offered a structure for godly living in a world where barbarians were in control. Reverend Timothy Fry, OSB, who edited an English edition of *The Rule of St Benedict*, wrote that Benedict's Rule "offered definitive direction and established an orderly way of life that gave security and stability. He sought to lay down 'nothing harsh, nothing burdensome' but was intent on encouraging the person coming to the monastery."[8]

Community Is Essential

All the practices of the Benedictines that resulted in a proliferation of art, literature, and science after the Dark Ages were tied to the strength of their community. Their commitment to grow together gave them the power to accomplish more than what one person or one family could achieve on their own. They weren't alone in their pursuit of God, and they had each other for support and encouragement. The same applies to every modern countercultural movement. In essence, every sect practicing a way of life that is different from the norm is able to continue because they aren't doing it alone. The demise of the Shakers is a good example of what happens when a well-meaning community grows too small to offer support. The Shakers were a religious group in America that left a legacy of beautiful craftsmanship, but their commitment to celibacy and avoidance of marriage eroded their community, which slowly died off. Without the growth that comes from expanding families, the Shaker community faded into history. We need people; we need the comfort, accountability, and support that a like-minded growing community can offer.

But people are messy, and some of you may have at times found yourself trapped in legalism and control, and it left you feeling scared to get close to people again. When we were a younger family, we found a community that we were drawn to. They shared our love for Jesus and our desire to be a close family. They also shared our love for missions, so they felt like our people, except that they also believed that celebrating Christmas was a sin, and they urged women to wear dresses at all times. There are many similar groups today, and if they are your people, enjoy! It's good to have values and ideas, and it's okay to be different from the rest of society. However, I personally still wanted to wear pants in freezing weather, and I still wanted to hang stockings for my children at Christmastime. It might have been fine for me to keep doing those things and hanging out with those people, but I didn't have the confidence to be with them while being different from them. I was waiting for the hammer of condemnation to drop, and the feeling that I was being judged by them made it uncomfortable to be a part of that group. I couldn't conform to their ideals, but I wasn't yet aware of how loved by God I am, so it created for me an irreconcilable difference. I wanted my warm jeans and Christmas stockings more than I wanted that community, and I wasn't sure enough of myself to try to have both.

I hope that you are more mature than I was then. I hope that you can discern the important values for your family and then find a community that supports those values, even if every choice is not the same within the community. We now have friends who have been able to forge that kind of community. They are in community with people who believe differently than they do about expressions of faith, and yet they are confident enough in themselves and their values to continue gathering and building a cohesive community despite small differences. The same can be true for you and me. We can be in close community with people who share some of our values but not all. We can agree to "major on the majors" and to have grace with each other as we "work out" our "own salvation with fear and trembling" (Philippians 2:12).

Avoid Isolation

Some of you have been in a supportive church or family, but then isolated yourself after getting unsolicited feedback. Several years ago, a friend complained about how an older woman at her church lectured her son about smoking. She was offended on behalf of her son and wanted to withdraw from that relationship. It is painful to receive criticism about our children, especially when we don't feel well-loved by the people giving the feedback. Some family relationships have broken down over unsolicited advice. Adult children grow weary of parents continually telling them what to do, and parents are so invested in their children's well-being that it is hard for them to refrain from giving advice—even when children are grown. But without feedback, we won't grow; a little pressure from extended family or church community isn't all bad if we can sift through it with a biblical filter and stand on truth.

I've been grateful over the years for my parents and siblings. They have given me plenty of feedback ranging from, "You need to make your kids clean under their beds," to "Your son used a bad word in a social media post." Getting advice was uncomfortable in the moment, and I wished that I could be perfect and avoid such feedback. However, in my busy life as a mom of many, I appreciated having people love me enough to share their insight. It's embarrassing and painful to receive bad news about our kids, and sometimes the opinions of others are just that, opinions and not necessarily an action item. But surrounding yourself with people who love you enough to speak into your life is an important part of a restoration home. Love isn't shown just through peaceful meals together and playdates. Love means caring enough to have hard conversations, and then staying in a relationship even if we don't agree. We need people, and conflict is the price of true community, so developing the grit to work through conflict and stay connected is essential.

How do we build these communities? Many people are simply moving to where they have discovered an existing group, choosing to fit into what is already being built. But for some of us, our home is our home. We want to stay close to the family and friends we already have. So how can we build a more cohesive community right where we are? I think the very first step is to discern what your values as a family are. Take time to write down what is important to you and what your own family vision is. I talk more about this in *Mothering by the Book*, and you can download a template for working through a family vision at https://www.ThePeacefulPreschool .com/blog/creating-a-family-vision. If you don't yet know what is important to you, it will be hard to build a community around it. When you take the time to evaluate the kind of life you want to build with your family, the way you want to spend your free time, and the character qualities you want to develop, you can begin to find people who also value those things.

There are many intangibles that I hold dear, like simple living, time in nature, self-sufficiency, prayer, worship, family time, and personal growth. We have found a community that shares those values. The way we parent our children is a little different, but for all of us, God is the center. We found this community by joining a private homeschool group forty-five minutes away in another small town. After two years of driving up the mountain for events with our group, or asking friends to drive down the hill to our home, we sold our house and moved up the hill. While it wasn't a big cross-country move, it did take effort to get into a community we loved. Some of the things that drew us to this place were the regular worship nights that people would host, and the hunger for God's presence that we witnessed in these people. We were also drawn to the natural beauty of our new home; we are surrounded by glorious mountain streams and lakes, and are near amazing hiking trails, so we can enjoy God inside and outside. The creativity in this community was another aspect that drew us. Many of the small businesses in our town are run by people who love their craft and pay attention to details, and we love that our children can work for these people and learn from them. And we were drawn to freedom. The families we hang out with truly want to live for God and to honor him in every aspect of their lives, but they are accepting of other people's journeys. They do not condemn others for choosing a different path. There is a love that overrides judgment, and so we can stay in community with each other, even if we have small disagreements on how to parent or spend our money or other personal decisions. We work together toward more holistic homes, better government, safer towns, and healthier churches—and we love each other.

> As we define our values as families, and center our lives in God's Word, we can find our people and together be a light in the world.

I know this sounds dreamy, but I believe there are similar communities all around the world, and more that can be created. You can find people to take meals to after childbirth who will do the same for you. You can find friends who will pray for your children with you. You can find friends to worship with, to learn with, and to love. We may not have the living example of disciplined Christians like Corrie ten Boom or the rigid structures of Esther Jungreis' Orthodox Judaism, but we can have something even better. As we define our values as families, and center our lives in God's Word, we can find our people and together be a light in the world. We can be a city set on a hill as we pursue God together.

STUDY GUIDE

What was the community like in your family of origin?

Did you have strong family traditions as a child?

What traditions do you cultivate in your own family?

How do you build a like-minded community?

Habits of Community: Choose a few of these habits to add to your own family rule, or brainstorm your own.

> Gather for worship.
> Define your values as a family.
> Discuss your values with close friends or established community.
> Define nonnegotiable values for strong community.
> Learn to give and receive feedback with grace.
> Learn to have boundaries for nonnegotiables.
> Be present with people during their times of need.
> Let people be present with you in your times of need.

What rule will your family adopt regarding community? For example:

> The _____ family lives by the Bible and cultivates community with similar values.
> The _____ family is available and present for friends in need.

Or write your own here:

_____

_____

When you have decided on your statement about habits of community, you can plug it into the Your Family Rule template in the appendix.

A VERSE TO MEMORIZE

Beloved, let us love one another, for love is from God, and whoever loves has been born of God and knows God.

1 John 4:7

A PRAYER

Dear God, thank you for creating us with a need for friends. Please forgive me for the times that I haven't treasured my friendships and for the ways I've made the opinions of friends more important than following your Word. Help me to develop friendships that are loving but also that help me grow in my faith. Help me to be a good friend. Amen

FURTHER READING

The Committed Life by Rebbetzin Esther Jungreis
Evidence Not Seen by Darlene Deibler Rose
In This House of Brede by Rumer Godden
Holy Hygge by Jamie Erickson

A RECIPE TO TRY

Challah Bread

1 cup lukewarm water
6 tablespoons melted butter
¼ cup honey
2 large eggs

1 tablespoon yeast
4 cups unbleached flour
1½ teaspoons salt

Glaze
1 large egg beaten with 1 tablespoon cold water

PREP: 30 minutes COOK: 40 minutes TOTAL: 70 minutes

1. Beat together water, butter, honey, and eggs.
2. Add yeast and mix well.
3. In a separate bowl, mix flour and salt together.
4. Stir in wet ingredients with a wooden spoon.
5. Knead until dough is smooth, about 6 minutes.
6. Cover and let rise in a warm place until doubled, about 1 hour.
7. Divide the dough into three pieces.
8. On a large baking sheet, stretch the dough into three 12-inch ropes and then braid together.
9. Coil the braid into a circle.
10. Allow to rise until doubled in size, about 45 minutes.
11. Preheat oven to 375°F. Beat glaze together and brush gently on bread.
12. Place loaf in hot oven with aluminum foil tent covering.
13. Bake for 40 minutes.

Serves 6

10

HABITS OF BALANCE

Madeleine L'Engle

The Son of God suffered unto death, not that men might not suffer, but that their sufferings might be like his.

Madeleine L'Engle, *Walking on Water*

We heard the sound faintly as we meandered up the narrow stone street. It was the rumbling of drums, and as we walked into the small plaza in the ancient city of Assisi, the instruments reached a crescendo, bringing smiles of joy as we experienced the drama and beauty of a drum parade in this beautiful Italian city. We were there for Christmas, and in awe of the experience. It was a season of deep connection and shared vision in our family, and a time of missional living together that was marked by joy. Just a year prior, we had traveled to Tanzania together with all seven of our children to co-lead a marriage conference for missionaries, and then we had gone to Colorado that summer to help care for children at a family camp. Now we were experiencing the city where Saint Francis started his ministry and spent his life.

We had long admired this humble saint, who gave up everything to follow God, so walking in his footsteps and praying in the places he prayed moved our hearts. It was thrilling to explore the stone paths where he had walked and talked with his brothers and sisters, encouraging them to be instruments of peace, to sow love instead of striving. And honestly, we were also moved by the food. We often started the day with panettone and coffee, followed by a croissant and cappuccino, and then had a simple lunch of fresh bread, cheese, and salami bought from the local grocer. We ate dinner in tiny restaurants tucked into the stone walls of the city, navigating the curving streets on foot to find them because it was a car-free city. For Christmas breakfast, I made our traditional cinnamon rolls in a tiny oven, purchasing the ingredients with a measure of faith since I couldn't really read the Italian labels. We were delighted by the amazing food, but we were also delighted by the presence of God in this ancient city. We could taste and see that the Lord is good, and His presence was a tangible flavor of joy. When we walked into the pilgrim chapel where people have been praying for a thousand years, you could feel the weighty atmosphere of those prayers as the Spirit of God saturated the place, and I was instantly moved to tears.

It wasn't all luxury, though. We were traveling with carry-on bags, so comforts from home were few, and our Italian Airbnb was cold and very, very old. The kitchen consisted of a two-burner stove, a table, and a stand-alone sink—and the landlady kept the interior temperature at a drafty 65 degrees. Although we only had tiny suitcases for a two-week stay, I had managed to hide a few Christmas presents in my bag, a stack of P.G. Wodehouse paperbacks that we all passed around, some Christmas candies, a Calico Critter or Playmobil for my youngest two, and new socks that filled in for stockings. We had little with us in the way of possessions or home comforts, but we took comfort in each other, and the time with God and the beautiful food made up for the thin, creaky beds and cold stone rooms.

We Are Loved

Part of what made this such a happy time in our family is that my identity issues had been settled with God. For many years I had believed a theology that said if I failed to be perfect then I wasn't saved, and so I was used to judging myself and others by this standard. It made life miserable to wonder if I was saved, and constantly feel pressure to perform in order to hang onto salvation. When we believe that God's grace is small and revocable, we tend to be on the lookout for ways other people have blown it in order to prop ourselves up, which also brought me great pain. When we think we could lose our salvation so easily, it creates competition instead of rest and peace. This creates an imbalance in the lives of believers, as instead of living in the joy and grace of the gospel, we live on a precarious perch, constantly judging instead of trusting that salvation belongs to the Lord. While there is certainly a call to be discerning, this is not the same as constantly speaking and thinking ill about others and condemning anyone with whom we differ on points of doctrine or belief. Discernment is very different from living closed off to others out of fear. After I recognized the beauty of salvation by faith alone, and began resting in my identity as the beloved, I could find balance and enjoy each day as it came.

The Benedictines had to find their equilibrium as well. They were welcoming new brothers into the fold who had been raised differently and who had a different experience of life and family. They had a rule to live by, yes, but they also had to consider the frailty of humanity and not set up standards that were impossible to meet. They had to cultivate a sense of joy in obedience without setting the brothers up for failure. In his prologue, Saint Benedict writes,

We propose, therefore, to establish a school of the Lord's service, and in setting it up we hope we shall lay down nothing that is harsh or hard to bear. But if for adequate reason for the correction of faults or the preservation of charity, some degree of restraint is laid down, do not then and there be overcome with terror, and run away from the way of salvation, for its beginning must needs be difficult. On the contrary, through the continual practice of monastic observance and the life of faith, our hearts are opened wide, and the way of God's commandments is run in a sweetness of love that is beyond words.[1]

Saint Benedict intended for there to be balance. He intended for the needs of the whole body to be met, and for the rule to be neither harsh, nor burdensome. And allowances are to be made to meet special needs,

Although human nature is of itself drawn to feel compassion for these life-periods, namely, old age and childhood, still, let the decree of the Rule make provision also for them. Let their natural weakness be always taken into account and let the strictness of the Rule not be kept with them in respect to food, but let there be a tender regard in their behalf and let them eat before regular hours.[2]

Even the rules regarding food had balance built in. If the brothers were working somewhere that was very hot, or working in the fields, they were permitted to eat earlier; if they were sick, they were permitted more wine. The structure was strong, but not rigid, built on kindness and a desire for the good of those who followed it. Their lives were not meant to be all preaching or all work, but a holistic cycle; work, study, pray, eat, rest—a cycle that nourishes body and soul.

And balance wasn't just required in the areas of food and care of the body. The abbot of the monastery (the monk chosen to lead) was required to have spiritual balance as well. Saint Benedict writes,

Let him be chaste, sober, and merciful, and let him always exalt "mercy above judgment" (Jas 2:13), that he also may obtain mercy.

Let him hate vice, but love the brethren. And even in his corrections, let him act with prudence and not go to extremes, lest, while he aimeth to remove the rust too thoroughly, the vessel be broken.[3]

So while as families we should pursue personal holiness and wholeness, we don't have to do it by stepping on other believers or even the other members of our family. Restoration doesn't happen by creating social media posts criticizing the faith journey of others. While discernment is important so we don't get absorbed into a falling world, discernment should help us grow in mercy toward others. If we are quick to judge others, it puts us in danger of being judged. We can remember Jesus' exhortation to "Judge not, that you be not judged. For with the judgment you pronounce you will be judged, and with the measure you use it will be measured to you" (Matthew 7:1–2).

The Struggle for Balance

Madeleine L'Engle understood this struggle. She was a Christian author who wrote the popular literary series *A Wrinkle in Time* along with many other fiction and nonfiction books for children and adults. She recognized that being a Christian in the world of artists was to be unpopular and misunderstood, but her faith was too much a part of her to diminish. She couldn't merely be a writer and leave Jesus out of it because he was integral to her very being. She was outspoken about her faith, but she also received criticism from other believers, putting her in a hard place where the secular world didn't want her because she was Christian, but many in the Christian world didn't want her because her books contained too much fantasy. She wrote, "In the world of literature, Christianity is no longer respectable. When I am referred to in an article or a review as a 'practicing Christian' it is seldom meant as a compliment, at least not in the secular press."[4]

Despite the opposition from the secular press, Madeleine remained a devoted Christian, whose life was characterized by dedication to daily Scripture reading and prayer. In her book on faith and art, *Walking on Water*, she writes of her daily disciplines, "No matter where I am, at home, abroad, I begin the day with morning prayer, including the psalms for the day, so that at the end of each month I have gone through the book of Psalms. I also read from both the Old and New Testaments."[5]

Sadly, many Christians became her biggest critics, instead of being a refuge and support for her. These Christian critics insisted on banning the books or made it their ambition to destroy her reputation; perhaps it was their fear and suspicion of the human imagination that made them hostile to her whimsical stories. In Sarah Arthur's book about the author's life, *A Light So Lovely*, she includes a speech during which Madeleine addressed these detractors:

> I don't understand Christians who are looking for hate. That is not Christlike. But, see, I have a real big problem here: How do I keep from being judgmental about people I think are judgmental? . . . But it does make me very sad. Because when I write something which I believe is an offering to God and it's seen as wicked, I say, "What have I done wrong? . . . Is that what the book says?" But then I get enough affirmation from other people saying, "No, that's not what the book says." There's something abroad today that frightens me that I've never seen before, in a group of people calling themselves Christians who want to put other Christians down, rather than uphold, teach, be witnesses.[6]

This is where that Benedictine balance is needed. As you pursue a restoration lifestyle, the temptation to judge those who are doing life differently is bound to crop up. As a young mom, I was guilty of this judgment. We were in a church with strict views about parenting and roles in marriage, and for an immature believer like myself, it led to my being very judgmental about people who were doing life with another value system. It's painful to remember how I criticized people and the perfectionistic culture I was trying to create. It was beautiful that I was reading the Bible every day to my children, that we weren't watching television, and that my children were polite and obedient, but my lack of mercy was just as sinful as being an apathetic parent. When my children did eventually throw a tantrum, or struggle to overcome a sin issue, all of that judgment was turned back on myself. I set myself up for failure by cultivating asceticism (severe self-discipline) in my home, and by judging others for their shortcomings as I saw them.

When Christians make a habit of criticizing and condemning other believers, whether it is over points of doctrinal difference, for their media choices, or how well they manage their household, we are putting ourselves in the line of fire. If, instead, we accept that our attempt to restore culture and create sacred homes will be marked by failure, and that our means of working toward restoration won't look exactly like our neighbor's, we can begin to embrace the beauty of the process. If we can each work out our own salvation with fear and trembling, and allow our friends and neighbors to have their own journey, we will reach the heavenly city with a vessel marked by failure, but marked also by the beauty of humility and grace. Justin Whitmel Earley, in his conclusion to *The Common Rule*, writes of the Japanese art form Kintsugi, in which a vessel's cracks are filled with gold, making the imperfections into a work of art:

> For those who focus inward—which is the legalistic gaze—failure destroys them. But look outward. Look for beauty, and you'll see that failure is making *you* the work of art. You are God's pot, with cracks inlaid with the gold of grace. You are more beautiful now because of the fault lines.[7]

So as we create a rule of life and live by it, and take the time to write down our values as a family and fight against the creeping nihilism in order to save the good, the true, and the beautiful, we must do it with grace for ourselves and for those who are not on the same path. Madeleine L'Engle embodied this grace in many ways. She was a devoted Christian with a rule of life, with attention to Christian structures and rhythms. She writes of these in *Walking on Water,* "I begin the day with morning prayer. . . . I end the day in the same way, with evening prayer and this gives the day a structure."[8]

However, even with those structures, she was open to questions, and she acknowledged that life is messy. Some of the other Christian women I have written about might be more inspirational in their purity of devotion and their unflagging virtue, women like Elisabeth Elliot and Amy Carmichael, who seem almost mythical. For someone like myself, who has been a mom long enough to have many regrets and a high awareness of my failures, Elisabeth Elliot can make me feel hopeless. How can I have a sacred home when I'm so inconsistent? How can I help my children restore a broken world when I can't even stick to a Bible reading plan? How can I teach my children virtue when swearing is so easy for me? Our awareness of the human condition can leave us in despair, but then there is Madeleine, faithfully plodding along with her daily Bible reading and regular church attendance and love for Jesus while her son drinks himself to death, her granddaughter is terribly injured in an accident, and she suffers her own physical ailments. She wrote, "George McDonald gives me renewed strength during times of trouble—times when I have seen people tempted to deny God—when he says, 'The Son of God suffered unto death, not that men might not suffer, but that their sufferings might be like his.'"[9]

Some of you may be in a suffering season right now. You may already have a list of regrets as a parent and wonder how restoration is possible for your own life, much less the world. Some of you may be dealing with addictions in your family, or children who have lost their way. The bright-eyed spark of your hopeful early days as a family is now mingled with cynicism and despair as the accumulation of your mistakes and theirs threatens to snowball and destroy everyone in its path. The days of pinafores and playdough have given way to hard conversations about dating and social media and how many piercings are acceptable, and you wonder how that mud pie-making child became so full of self-hatred. You may have tried everything to bring restoration to this situation—seeking counsel, getting the right combination of vitamins, grieving your lost childhood, and forgiving those who have offended you—and still the breakthrough you are so desperate for lingers just out of reach. The last few years have ground away at all of us, and many of you might be ready to check out altogether. To check out on being a mom, to check out on being a wife, maybe even to check out on life.

You are not alone in your discouragement. The recent years have held so many hard moments for our family, including lost jobs and subsequent erosion of confidence, relational conflicts, and illness. As well, the increase in homelessness and suicide and threats of war and inflation in the larger world all threaten to overwhelm us. Through both the inner turmoil and external circumstances, this awareness has given me strength: *The little things we do matter, and they continue to matter.* The Psalm verse that has been encouraging me is this one: "Trust in the LORD and do good; dwell in the land and enjoy safe pasture" (Psalm 37:3 NIV).

It is faithfulness that makes the difference. It's not the big breakthroughs that ultimately carry us through, although we should still hope for them. It's not miracles that we rely on, although we still pray for God to show up supernaturally. But when the big breakthroughs and instant deliverance from our failures don't come, it's still choosing day after day to do our best that brings restoration. It's choosing to continue to trust in God's Word even when his people have let you down. It's choosing to continue the spiritual disciplines even if you are still battling the same vices that you've battled for so long. It's choosing to feed yourself healthy food and live with healthy structure, and invite Jesus into the trauma of your childhood when numbing out would be easier. Life is messy, we will make mistakes, our children will make mistakes, and bad things will happen despite our best efforts—but good things are happening too. When we keep faithfully trusting in God and doing good, there will be a reward. Whether we see the fruit of sowing peace in this life or the next is up to God, but he promises to reward those who diligently seek him (Hebrews 11:6), and he always honors his Word. The temptation when we don't see the immediate fruit of our efforts is to throw in the towel and join the nihilists, drinking and partying because tomorrow we all may die, but remember these words of God: "You make known to me the path of life; in your presence there is fullness of joy; at your right hand are pleasures forevermore" (Psalm 16:11). Instead of giving up when you suffer, keep your life in balance, knowing that true joy is found in intimate relationship with God. So stay on the path of joy, neither judging people for what they don't know, nor joining the debauched in their carelessness, but instead keeping your eyes fixed on Jesus.

Ultimately, obtaining a sense of balance, that happy place where you are doing your best to follow the rules but also enjoying your life and not judging others, comes down to knowing the gospel. We're given instruction in God's Word about how to live, and we've been given a clear picture of what is in store for those who obey. God promises good to those who obey him:

> Therefore shall ye keep all the commandment which I command thee this day, that ye may be strong, and go in and possess the land, whither ye go over to possess it; and that ye may prolong your days in the land, which Jehovah sware unto your fathers to give unto them and to their seed, a land flowing with milk and honey.
>
> Deuteronomy 11:8–9 ASV

There is also God's promise to destroy those who disobey and persist in sin:

> And it shall be, if thou shalt forget Jehovah thy God, and walk after other gods, and serve them, and worship them, I testify against you this day that ye shall surely perish. As the nations that Jehovah maketh to perish before you, so shall ye perish; because ye would not hearken unto the voice of Jehovah your God.
>
> Deuteronomy 8:19–20 ASV

The book of Deuteronomy is a continual reminder of the blessing of obedience; and yet we will fail because, in fact, "all have sinned and fall short of the glory of God" (Romans 3:23).

In my days as a Christian before I understood the gospel of salvation through grace by faith, I thought it was all up to me, and I lived in fear of making mistakes. Such fearful living steals joy and tempts us to judge others. Jinger Vuolo writes of a similar struggle in her book *Becoming Free Indeed*. She writes, "I was consumed with being introspective, overcome by paranoia. I obsessively dissected my life—my thoughts, words, and actions—because I was terrified that a sin might sneak in and cause me to lose God's blessings. If I forgot to ask forgiveness for a single sin, I felt condemned."[10]

Her experience of Christianity without the gospel made her believe that every outcome was up to her obedience and performance, and this had characterized my life as well. This stole all the joy of being a child of God from me and added fear to my life as I constantly worried about making a wrong move. Once I understood that the work that Jesus did on the cross covered all my mistakes, past and future, it changed everything. I am no longer obsessed about what people think of me. Now I recognize that I am a child of God, restored to the position that Adam and Eve enjoyed in the garden, the position of intimacy with God, enjoying being his child instead of trying to earn his love. This made it easy to obey, but it also made it easy to just enjoy him. It restored a sense of childlike faith. Young children aren't constantly performing for love; rather, the need to perform for love starts after they've been wounded. In their innocence, they are fun and cute and occasionally naughty, but they still trust that they will be loved no matter what. It's when they start to make mistakes and feel that love is withdrawn, or they give us a picture they drew and we brush it off, that the pressure of trying to earn love creeps in. But Jesus isn't like our earthly parents. He is merciful, and he celebrates us. "The Lord your God in your midst, The Mighty One, will save; He will rejoice over you with gladness, He will quiet you with His love, He will rejoice over you with singing" (Zephaniah 3:17).

> Now I recognize that I am a child of God, restored to the position that Adam and Eve enjoyed in the garden, the position of intimacy with God, enjoying being his child instead of trying to earn his love.

With this new awareness, everything shifted. With this newfound freedom, I didn't start getting high everyday just because I was saved by the gospel and not my works. I didn't start partying with friends every weekend and living my life in a drunken stupor. I didn't start running away from my children, burying myself in social media to escape the inevitable sense of inadequacy that mothering brings. Those are things we do when we want to escape ourselves, not things that the beloved do. Knowing I was loved and safe and that my sins were covered made me want to live a clean life. It made me want to read God's Word and snuggle close to him. It made me want to love my husband and my children. It made me want to care for my home and grow a garden and love my neighbors. It made me want to take my vitamins, and care for my health and my heart, to pursue wholeness in every area of my life.

It made me want to live a life that brings restoration and creates a sacred home for God to inhabit. Now the motivation was from a place of being loved instead of trying to earn love. I wasn't trying to save the world under my own power, but rather just to be the beloved, and being the beloved naturally leads to restoration. My hunger to live intentionally was motivated by a regenerated heart and not fear of punishment. It was motivated by delight.

Mercy Triumphs over Judgment

And I suppose therein lies the hinge for restoration of our homes and culture. If we are doing it out of fear or with a spirit of anger and judgment toward the wicked, we will reap the fruit of that anger. If we are doing it in pride, thinking we are better than others, God will resist us. This emphasis on judging others only ends up bringing more judgment on ourselves. This leads to a shame spiral, where in a heightened awareness of our failures, we give up on the pursuit of the better. However, when we pursue God, and live by a rule of life that honors him with the simple motivation of love, the fruit will inevitably be love—but with hearts fixed on God and trusting in God, the fruit won't be our primary concern. We won't be fixated on how well we did or didn't do, because we are covered in the righteousness of Christ. No longer are we trying to prove ourselves by our behavior, but we are simply being obedient out of love. We are the clay, not the potter; when in loving submission we throw ourselves on the mercy of the Potter who is also the Good Shepherd, we can trust that he will be with us and will never leave us or forsake us. It is his presence that creates a sacred home, not our work. Our habits are just what we do as a response to his love.

When I was nearly finished writing this book, I read a biography of Saint Benedict. Until then, I had focused my research on the Rule, but reading his life story brought a new perspective. He didn't start his ministry by writing a list of rules. Instead, he spent three years living in a cave, in communion with God. He devoted himself to loving and being loved by God, because it's through intimacy with him that the power to obey comes. Benedict's ministry was marked by power. All of this devotion to God led to supernatural living in a time in history when murderous barbarians roamed the land and famine was destroying people. Through this distressing time, God provided miraculously for Benedict and his brothers. When the oil ran out, God refilled the barrel, and when sickness struck them, God raised the dead. The needs at that time were great, but the power of God was greater. Benedict had intimacy with God cultivated through daily practices of prayer, and this intimacy helped him live by the rule. As well, this intimacy gave him the wisdom to respond to trials with grace and insight.

> It is his presence that creates a sacred home, not our work. Our habits are just what we do as a response to his love.

The world might feel dark and chaotic, the news increasingly scary, and the experiences of your own family traumatic and sad, but restoration is coming. The Benedictines lived through similarly uncertain times, and yet the foundation they laid for the simple pursuit of God changed the world. Our work is changing the world as well, one simple home at a time. It's true, God is preparing new bodies and new homes and a new earth for us. We can't even imagine the goodness God is preparing for us. So as we wait for his redemption, we are imitating our Heavenly Father as we work toward restoration of homes that honor his sacred Presence—toward His Kingdom come, His will being done here on earth as it is in heaven.

So take your order and prayer, your work and simplicity and stewardship, take community and hospitality and add in stability and balance, and create a rule to live by. Start with just one small step at a time; maybe it will be morning and evening prayers, or inviting a neighbor over once a week, or teaching your children to follow directions. Do that one step for a week and then add another structure to your life. Get started, and when you fail (which happens to all of us), don't let shame and judgment derail you. Instead, forgive yourself and start again. Start living with faithful diligence, not giving up when it's hard, and not trying to do too much at once. Stay steady on the path of God's commandments. Start living with this beautiful simplicity, and let God do a miracle with your mustard seed of faith.

> We shall run on the path of God's commandments, our hearts overflowing with the inexpressible delight of love.
>
> Rule of St. Benedict, Prologue 49

STUDY GUIDE

Why is balance needed in our pursuit of restoration?

How do feelings of pride or failure sabotage our efforts?

In previous chapters you developed a set of statements about the values and habits you want to focus on. You can find a Canva template to make a printable poster to remind your family of the values you want to pursue at https://shorturl.at/hnK01.

A VERSE TO MEMORIZE

Eye has not seen, nor ear heard,
Nor have entered into the heart of man
The things which God has prepared for those who love Him.

1 Corinthians 2:9 NKJV

A PRAYER

Dear God, thank you that you have given us directions to follow, but you also know that we fail. Thank you that the path of salvation is not our good works but is the redemption that Jesus purchased for us on the cross. Help me to never take my eyes off Jesus. Help me to obey you not out of shame or condemnation but out of love. Please forgive me for the ways I have judged myself and others instead of living in your mercy. Let me be your vessel of honor, Lord. Amen

FURTHER READING

Walking on Water by Madeleine L'Engle
How to Stop the Pain by Dr. James B. Richards
Mothering by the Book by Jennifer Pepito
The Common Rule by Justin Whitmel Earley

A RECIPE TO TRY

Hot Cocoa

4 cups milk   ¼ cup sugar
½ cup cocoa powder   1 teaspoon vanilla

PREP: 5 minutes COOK: 10 minutes TOTAL: 15 minutes

1. Mix all ingredients in a heavy kettle.
2. Cook over medium low heat until warm and completely mixed.
3. Serve with marshmallows or whipped cream.

Serves 4

ACKNOWLEDGMENTS

The Peaceful Press and Restoration Home community of mothers, with their enthusiasm and bravery, have made the early morning writing sessions a joyful sacrifice. Hearing stories of how the trajectory of their families changed because of my work has infused me with strength when I felt the tug to give up my writing in favor of more time in nature with my children. As I think of each one of you diligently loving your children despite what is happening in the world, and keeping your homes and communities with such faithfulness, I'm inspired in my own journey. Your labor is not in vain.

Beloved Peaceful Press team, Emelie Pepito, Kristin Dahman, Angie Warren, Sadie Davis, Beth Ann Menger, and Brianna Rodriguez, you lighten my load so I can add book writing to curriculum creating. Your creativity and ingenuity make the Peaceful Press resources beautiful and lifegiving and it's an honor to partner with you in empowering homeschool families to love their children well.

Thank you, Ingrid Beck, for your insight and support. Having your advocacy and talent to help me navigate book publishing has been an incredible blessing.

To the team at Bethany House including Jennifer Dukes Lee, Stephanie Smith, Rebecca Schriner, and Sharon Hodge, it's been so much fun to work with you all. You are insightful and kind, and we share a love of God and prayer that makes publishing with you a dream. I love being part of the Bethany House family.

My Wild + Free friends have opened my world to new perspectives and so much fun. I've loved learning from Leah Boden, Greta Eskridge, Rea Berg, Betsy Larkin, Amber O'Neal Johnston, Leslie Martino, Erin Loechner, Elsie Iudicello, Richele Baburina, Tina Ingold, Jenni Dowling, Julie Bogart, Stephanie Beaty, and so many others. You are amazing women, and I'm delighted to be your friend. I'm so grateful to Ainsley Arment for inviting me into this magical community; so many of my best memories have been with you, whether it was kayaking down the Brazos River after Wild + Free Wimberley, snuggling in the hotel lobby after countless conferences, or eating beautiful lunches with my heroes, friendship with you has been a delight.

Sally Clarkson, a chapter in this book could have been written about you. Your faithfulness to continue highlighting the sacred work of motherhood has encouraged so many, and I'm grateful that in a world where older women often give up on Titus 2 mentorship, you continue to love and serve. I'm honored to be your friend.

Amy Hughes, thanks for being a gentle, loving presence in my life.

To Ginny Yurich, your sparkling personality has been a wonder to behold, and your generosity and calm are life changing. I'm so glad we are friends.

Rachel Kovac, thank you for deep conversations, thoughtful questions, and your beautiful presence. I've learned so much from you, everything you do is infused with love, and I'm honored to know you.

To Cindy Rollins, your willingness to be honest about the struggles of motherhood and yet hopeful about the importance of our work has impacted me deeply. Thank you for helping me keep going even when it's hard.

Cristina Eklund, I love watching the way you beautify your surroundings and raise your children with hope and faith. Your excitement about this project has been an inspiration.

To my Voxer friends Kate Crocco, Erin Cox, Cindy West, and Alicia Hutchinson. Thanks for bearing my burdens, sharing yours, and being models of motherhood and business. I'm so glad we are friends.

To my Rooted Home sisters, Aimee Kirk, Camille Fielder, Jessica Wilson, Stephanie Frediani, and Whitney Byrd, you are all so lovely and inspiring. I have hope for the world as I see the ways you are transforming our small corner of it.

To Melissa Wingo, thank you for helping me process these ideas through our weekly walks, and for challenging me when my tinfoil hat gets too big. I am so grateful for you.

To my sisters, Jacqueline Lostritto, Jody Kniesel, Tammi Gyori, and LeeAnn Gyori. You are wonderful mothers to many. You glorify God through your work and encourage me with your love.

To my parents, John and Rosalind Gyori, I'm so inspired by the ways you have exhibited great faith and virtue. Your diligence and grit have made your children capable and given me hope for the world.

To my children, Emelie, Eden, Elias, Ethan, Emmett, Ella, and Ezra, I love being your mom. You are all so beautiful and thoughtful, and I'm so proud of the ways you pursue God. You inspire me, and I'm so thankful that we get to grow together.

To Karina, thank you for being such a good friend to my son. You are a gift from God.

To my granddaughter Sylvia, I love you; you are precious to me.

To my husband, Scott, I love the way you pray, and I'm so thankful for your commitment to God and to your family. I'm so happy I get to spend my life with you.

I'm so grateful to you, God. The gift of your presence continues to empower me to love even when it is hard, and to be faithful even when the world is chaotic. Thank you for the comfort of your Word, and for the beauty of creation, and for your constant love and grace. I'm so glad I get to be your child and spend eternity with you.

YOUR RULE OF LIFE

On the following pages, write in the statements you developed at the end of each chapter—the practices your family will adopt for each habit to create your own family rule. You can also access an online template to fill in and print out at https://shorturl.at/BFJP0.

HABITS FOR
A SACRED HOME

Habits of Work:

_____

_____

_____

_____

_____

Habits of Stewardship:

_____

_____

_____

_____

Habits of Prayer:

_____

_____

Habits of Order:

Habits of Simplicity:

Habits of Stability:

Habits of Hospitality:

_____

_____

_____

_____

_____

Habits of Community:

_____

_____

_____

_____

_____

Habits of Balance:

_____

_____

_____

_____

_____

NOTES

Chapter 1: The Need for Sacred Homes

1. St. Gregory the Great, *The Life and Miracles of St. Benedict*, ed. Dom Edmund J. Luck, O.S.B. (London: R. Washbourne, 1880), 5.

2. Rod Dreher, *The Benedict Option: A Strategy for Christians in a Post-Christian Nation* (Sentinel: New York, 2017), 9, 12.

3. Francis Schaeffer, *A Christian Manifesto* (Wheaton, IL: Crossway, 1981), 17.

4. Stephanie Kramer, "U.S. Has World's Highest Rate of Children Living in Single-Parent Households," Pew Research Center, May 28, 2021, www.pew research.org/short-reads/2019/12/12/u-s-children-more-likely-than-children-in -other-countries-to-live-with-just-one-parent/.

5. D. Brewer, ed., *Quotes of Confucius and Their Interpretations, a Words of Wisdom Collection Book* (Lulu.com, 2020), 153.

Chapter 2: Habits of Work: Edith Schaeffer

1. Edith Schaeffer, *L'Abri* (Wheaton, IL: Tyndale House, 1971), 155–156.

2. Os Guinness, "Fathers and Sons: On Francis Schaeffer, Frank Schaeffer, and Crazy for God," Books & Culture, *Christianity Today*, March/April 2008, https://www.booksandculture.com/articles/2008/marapr/1.32.html?paging=off.

3. Aaron De Smet, Bonnie Dowling, Marino Mugayar-Baldocchi, Joachim Talloen, "The Great Attrition: Facing the Labor Shortage Conundrum," *McKinsey & Company*, December 6, 2021, https://www.mckinsey.com/capabilities/people -and-organizational-performance/our-insights/the-organization-blog/the-great -attrition-facing-the-labor-shortage-conundrum.

4. Margaret MacMillan, "Rebuilding the World After the Second World War," *Guardian* (US Edition), September 11, 2009, https://www.theguardian.com/world /2009/sep/11/second-world-war-rebuilding.

5. Michael David Knowles, "St. Benedict, Italian Monk," *Britannica*, updated August 1, 2013, https://www.britannica.com/biography/Saint-Benedict-of-Nursia.

6. Edith Schaeffer, *The Hidden Art of Homemaking* (Wheaton, IL: Tyndale House, 1971), 21.

7. Susan Schaeffer Macaulay, *For the Family's Sake* (Wheaton, IL: Crossway, 1999), 230.

8. Edith Schaeffer, *Ten Things Parents Must Teach Their Children* (Grand Rapids, MI: Baker Publishing, 1994), 102.

9. Frank Schaeffer, "A Tribute to My Evangelical Leader Mom—Edith Schaeffer RIP," *Huffpost*, March 30, 2013, https://www.huffpost.com/entry/a-tribute-to-my-evangelic_b_2983906.

10. Wendell Kimbrough, Paul Zach, and Isaac Wardell, "Your Labor Is Not in Vain" © 2017 Porter's Gate Publishing (BMI), Hymns from The Porter's Gate (ASCAP) and Porter's Gate Publications (SESAC).

Chapter 3: Habits of Stewardship: Mary McLeod Bethune

1. Sarah Maia Conde Pooner, "Why Rome Fell and Is the United States Next?," *Yale National Initiative to Strengthen Teaching in Public Schools*, n.d., https://teachers.yale.edu/curriculum/viewer/initiative_08.03.07_u#:~:text=Decline%20in%20Morals%20and%20Values&text=Many%20historians%20note%20that%20the,lavish%20overindulgent%20parties%2C%20and%20violence.

2. Saint Benedict, *The Rule of Saint Benedict in English* (Collegeville, MN: Liturgical Press, 1981, 2019), 55.

3. Emma Gelders Sterne, *Mary McLeod Bethune* (New York: Alfred A. Knopf, 1957), 42.

4. Sterne, *Mary McLeod Bethune*, 43.

5. "Dr. Mary McLeod Bethune," *Bethune–Cookman University,* https://www.cookman.edu/history/our-founder.html.

6. Debra Michals, ed., "Mary McLeod Bethune," *National Women's History Museum*, 2015, www.womenshistory.org/education-resources/biographies/mary-mcleod-bethune.

7. Tish Harrison Warren, *Liturgy of the Ordinary* (Downers Grove, IL: IVP Books, 2016), 31.

8. "Shorter Catechism of the Assembly of Divines: The 1647 Westminster Confession and Subordinate Documents," *A Puritan's Mind*, n.d., https://www.apuritansmind.com/westminster-standards/shorter-catechism/.

Chapter 4: Habits of Prayer: Amy Carmichael

1. Saint Benedict, *The Rule of St. Benedict in English* (Collegeville, MN: Liturgical Press, 1981, 2019), 47.

2. Ronald Rolheiser, *Domestic Monastery* (Brewster, MA: Paraclete Press, 2019), 9.

3. Ben Sansburn, "Amy Carmichael: 'Amma' to the Motherless," *Summit Christian Fellowship*, January 9, 2020, https://summit-christian.org/blog/2020/01/09/amy-carmichael-amma-to-the-motherless.

4. Amy Wilson-Carmichael, *Things as They Are: Mission Work in Southern India* (London: Morgan and Scott, 1905), 258.

5. Amy Carmichael, *Candles in the Dark: Letters of Hope and Encouragement* (Fort Washington, PA: CLC Publishing, 1981), 17.

6. Amy Carmichael, *Edges of His Ways* (Fort Washington, PA: Christian Literature Crusade, 1955, 2011), 18.

7. Tyler Staton, *Praying Like Monks, Living Like Fools* (Michigan: Zondervan, 2022), 124.

8. Eugene Peterson, *Run with the Horses: The Quest for Life at Its Best* (Downers Grove, IL: Intervarsity Press, 2019), 103.

9. Carmichael, *Candles in the Dark*, 113.

10. "For Our Children" from *Toward Jerusalem* by Amy Carmichael © 1936, renewed 1977 by The Dohnavur Fellowship, and published by CLC Publications, Fort Washington, PA. Used with permission.

Chapter 5: Habits of Order: Elisabeth Elliot

1. "What Is Autonomy and Why Does It Matter?," I.Family Project, November 11, 2014, https://www.ifamilystudy.eu/what-is-autonomy-and-why-does-it-matter/.

2. Saint Benedict, *The Rule of St. Benedict in English* (Collegeville, MN: Liturgical Press, 1981, 2019), 19.

3. Susan Schaeffer Macaulay, *For the Family's Sake* (Wheaton, IL: Crossway, 1999), 46.

4. Richard Weikart, "Marx, Engels, and the Abolition of the Family," History of European Ideas 18, no. 5 (1994): 657-672.

5. Saul D. Alinsky, *Rules for Radicals: A Practical Primer for Realistic Radicals* (New York: Vintage Books, 1972), 128.

6. Macaulay, *For the Family's Sake*, 47.

7. Elisabeth Elliot, *Joyful Surrender: 7 Disciplines for the Believer's Life* (Grand Rapids, MI: Revell, 1982), 25.

8. Jim Elliot journal entry, October 28, 1949, scanned image posted by Kevin Halloran, "Jim Elliot's Journal Entry with 'He Is No Fool...' Quote," Anchored in Christ blog, October 28, 2013, https://www.kevinhalloran.net/jim-elliot-quote-he-is-no-fool/.

9. Elliot, *Joyful Surrender*, 149–150.

10. Saint Benedict, *The Rule of St. Benedict in English*, 29.

11. Dennis Okholm, *Monk Habits for Everyday People* (Grand Rapids, MI: Brazos Press, 2007), 55.

12. Saint Benedict, *The Rule of Saint Benedict in English*, 24.

Chapter 6: Habits of Simplicity: Sabina Wurmbrand

1. Saint Benedict, *The Rule of Saint Benedict: Translated with an Introduction by Abbot Gasquet* (London: Chatto and Windus, 1909), 56.

2. R. Scott Clark, "Heidelberg Catechism (1563)," *The Heidelblog*, September 1, 2012, https://rscottclark.org/2012/09/heidelberg-catechism-1563/.

3. Sabina Wurmbrand, *The Pastor's Wife* (Bartlesville, OK: Living Sacrifice Book Company, 1970, 1989), 27.

4. Wurmbrand, *The Pastor's Wife*, 27–28.

5. Wurmbrand, *The Pastor's Wife*, 144.

6. Wurmbrand, *The Pastor's Wife*, 55.

7. Gerald G. May, MD, *Addiction and Grace: Love and Spirituality in the Healing of Addictions* (San Francisco: Harper & Rowe, 1988), 181.

Chapter 7: Habits of Stability: Ruth Bell Graham

1. *Merriam-Webster.com Dictionary*, s.v. "stability," accessed October 10, 2023, https://www.merriam-webster.com/dictionary/stability.

2. Saint Benedict, *The Rule of Saint Benedict in English,* 79.

3. Tony Klemmer, "A Visible Mark upon the Earth: Why Wendell Berry," Aspen Institute, May 18, 2020, https://www.aspeninstitute.org/blog-posts/why -wendell-berry/.

4. Wendell Berry, quoted in M.A. Grubbs, "Wendell Berry: People, Land and Fidelity," *Border States: Journal of the Kentucky-Tennessee American Studies Association*, no. 10 (1995), https://www.mtsu.edu/borders/archives/10/Wendell _Berry_-_People__Land_and_Fidelity.pdf.

5. Ruth Bell Graham as quoted in Patricia Cornwell, *A Time for Remembering: The Story of Ruth Bell Graham* (New York: Harper and Row, 1986), 67–68.

6. Billy Graham as quoted in Naomi Balk, "10 Things You May Not Know about Ruth Bell Graham," Billy Graham Evangelistic Association, June 14, 2022, https://billygraham.org/story/10-fun-facts-about-ruth-bell-graham/.

7. Roger Mitchell, "Angela Duckworth: The Power of Grit," Enterprising Investor, CFA Institute, July 15, 2022, https://blogs.cfainstitute.org/investor/2022 /07/15/angela-duckworth-the-power-of-grit/.

8. Gigi Graham as quoted in BGEA Admin, "Ruth Bell Graham: The Life of a Mother," Billy Graham Evangelistic Association, June 13, 2019, https://billy graham.org/gallery/ruth-bell-graham-the-life-of-a-mother/.

9. Betsy Larkin, personal note to Jennifer Pepito, 2022, used with permission.

10. Ned Graham as quoted in BGEA Admin, "Ruth Bell Graham: The Life of a Mother."

Chapter 8: Habits of Hospitality: Ella Tweten

1. Saint Benedict, *The Rule of St. Benedict in English* (Collegeville, MN: Liturgical Press, 1981, 2019), 73.

2. Margaret Jensen, *First We Have Coffee* (San Bernadino, CA: Here's Life Publishers, 1982), 56.

3. Jensen, *First We Have Coffee*, 56.

4. Jensen, *First We Have Coffee*, 51.

5. Jensen, *First We Have Coffee*, 120.

6. Esther de Waal, *Seeking God: The Way of St. Benedict* (Collegeville, MN: The Liturgical Press, 1984), 121.

7. Jensen, *First We Have Coffee*, 48.

8. Justin Whitmel Earley, *Habits of the Household: Practicing the Story of God in Everyday Family Rhythms* (Grand Rapids, MI: Zondervan, 2021), 61, 62.

9. Tyler Staton, *Praying Like Monks, Living Like Fools* (Grand Rapids, MI: Zondervan, 2022), 230.

Chapter 9: Habits of Community: Esther Jungreis

1. Corrie ten Boom, *The Hiding Place* (New York: Bantam Books, 1974), 194.

2. Ten Boom, *The Hiding Place*, 134–135.

3. Ten Boom, *The Hiding Place*, 194.

4. William Grimes, "Esther Jungreis, 'the Jewish Billy Graham,' Dies at 80," *New York Times*, August 26, 2016, https://www.nytimes.com/2016/08/26/nyregion /esther-jungreis-known-as-the-jewish-billy-graham-dies-at-80.html.

5. Rebbetzin Esther Jungreis, *The Committed Life* (New York: Cliff Street Books, 1998), 277.

6. Jungreis, *The Committed Life*, xiii.

7. Jungreis, *The Committed Life*, xv.

8. Saint Benedict, *The Rule of St. Benedict in English*, 11.

Chapter 10: Habits of Balance: Madeleine L'Engle

1. Abbot Parry OSB, trans., *The Rule of St. Benedict* (Herefordshire, UK: Gracewing, 1990), 4.

2. Rev. Boniface Verheyen, *The Holy Rule of St. Benedict* (Grand Rapids, MI: Christian Classics Ethereal Library), 47.

3. Verheyen, *The Rule of St. Benedict* in English, 76.

4. Madeleine L'Engle, *Walking on Water* (New York: Convergent Books, 1980), 51.

5. L'Engle, *Walking on Water*, 162.

6. Madeleine L'Engle, quoted in Sarah Arthur, *A Light So Lovely: The Spiritual Legacy of Madeleine L'Engle, Author of a Wrinkle in Time* (Grand Rapids, MI: Zondervan, 2018), 179.

7. Justin Whitmel Earley, *The Common Rule: Habit of Purpose for an Age of Distraction* (Illinois: InterVarsity Press, 2019), 166.

8. L'Engle, *Walking on Water*, 162.

9. L'Engle, *Walking on Water*, 17.

10. Jinger Duggar Vuolo, *Becoming Free Indeed: My Story of Disentangling Faith from Fear* (Nashville, TN: Thomas Nelson, 2023), 55.

JENNIFER PEPITO is the host of the *Restoration Home* podcast, author of *Mothering by the Book*, and the founder of The Peaceful Press (ThePeacefulPress.com). Jennifer is on a mission to help moms overcome fear and live with wonder and purpose, and her homeschool curriculum empowers this through heroic stories, heartwarming poetry, and engaging life skills development. Her resources help create joyful memories among families, which lead to deeper connections and lasting relationships. Jennifer's writing has been featured in several online and print journals, including *Wild + Free*, *Commonplace Quarterly*, and *Home Educating Family*. She hosted the *Wild + Free* podcast for seven years and has made guest appearances on other popular podcasts such as *1000 Hours Outside*, *At Home with Sally*, and *Read Aloud Revival*. Jennifer lives with her beloved family in the mountains, where she enjoys reading aloud, working in her garden, and watching the sunset.